Yo

Hexagonie, Part 1

An Innovative Way to Teach French

Maria Rice-Jones

Brilliant
PUBLICATIONS

About the author

Maria Rice-Jones is a French national with a Masters Degree in Modern Languages from the Sorbonne University in Paris. Since 1990, she has taught French to students of primary level and above in Paris, Milan and London.

Published by
Brilliant Publications
Unit 10
Sparrow Hall Farm
Edlesborough
Dunstable
Bedfordshire LU6 2ES

Written by Maria Rice-Jones
Illustrated by Sarah Wimperis
Designed by Z2 Ltd

ISBN 978 1 905780 59 4 (This book is sold together with a CD. The individual items are not available separately.)
A set of flashcards to accompany the book is also available (ISBN 978 1 905780 60 0)
First published in the UK 2009.
10 9 8 7 6 5 4 3 2 1

Contents

From the author

Hexagonie is designed for non-specialist and specialist teachers of French in primary schools. It offers a fresh and creative approach to teaching French and is presented in a logical, easy-to-follow format. Whatever their experience with the French language, *Hexagonie* will enable teachers to achieve material results in the classroom. The fast-paced lessons, with an emphasis on learning and using language structures, enable pupils to rapidly demonstrate the ability to communicate and converse with confidence.

I have been developing, trialing and testing the *Hexagonie* method over many years for use in my own classroom. It has now been formalized as a book at the encouragement of my pupils and colleagues. *Hexagonie* is guided by my own personal quest to challenge the "difficulties" of the French language head-on with a bold and imaginative teaching style that makes learning French easier and more accessible than is typically possible with many French schemes or textbooks. A key principle of the *Hexagonie* method is that parrot-style learning of grammatical rules and vocabulary lists should be avoided because it is laborious, and what is learned is often quickly forgotten. Instead, my approach to learning makes learning French enjoyable. It encourages children to play with words and language structures and to create their own memory techniques, which in turn help them to internalize the language, making them more efficient learners.

Hexagonie is a highly systematic "synthetic" approach to teaching French. Elements of language are carefully introduced, one step at a time, so that each unit builds on what has been learned before. So, for example, children are introduced to only the indefinite article ("a") in Unit 1. With this building block and the introduction of "c'est" in Unit 2 they can then start to build their own sentences and enjoy the rewards of being able to communicate in a foreign language. Each unit builds on the pupils' cumulative knowledge, thus building a firm foundation.

Hexagonie integrates a wide range of interesting facts about French and the French way of life so that pupils will gain a rich insight into the culture and diversity of the country.

Hexagonie will make you see French in a different light and help you to teach more creatively and efficiently. This is what *Hexagonie* is all about.

Enjoy!

Maria Rice-Jones

Teaching using the Hexagonie method

Hexagonie is a two-part scheme for teaching French to 7-11 year olds. *Hexagonie, Part 1* is for use with pupils in Years 3 and 4 (or later, depending on when they start French) and *Hexagonie, Part 2* is for use with pupils in Years 5 and 6.

Hexagonie, Part 1 consists of:
- Book containing lesson plans and photocopiable sheets
- Audio CD

A set of 120 colour flashcards to accompany the book is also available.

Structure of the units

There are 15 units in *Hexagonie, Part 1*. As each unit builds on the preceding one, the units need to be taught in order. However, it is up to you, the teacher, to decide how many lessons to split the units into. The units are subdivided so there are convenient breaking points. We haven't provided rigid lesson plans as the time available and pace in which pupils can work will differ from class to class. Each unit provides a detailed lesson plan and related photocopiable pupil sheets.

Bonjour and au revoir

We recommend that you begin each lesson with "Bonjour" and end with "Au revoir". Greeting people politely is a very important part of French culture, and taking the time to greet the children at the start of the lesson and say a formal goodbye at the end will reinforce this.

Hexagonie story

In each unit you will find a story, written in English, about the imaginary land of "Hexagonie". These stories are designed to be read aloud, either by you or by pupils, and then discussed. The imaginary land of Hexagonie gets its name from the shape of France. In fact, many French people refer to France as "l'hexagone". The inhabitants of Hexagonie are parts of speech: nouns, verbs, etc. These fun stories reinforce key teaching points. They work in much the same way as the "memory tricks", helping to engage pupils' imaginations and encourage learning. Pupils could be encouraged to keep their copies of the stories and make them into a little booklet.

Recap on previous units

Each unit (after Unit 1) starts with a recap on what has been learned in the preceding lesson. If you split up the units into smaller segments, we recommend that you begin each lesson with a quick oral recap of what you did the lesson before.

Essential words and phrases

Each unit has a list of essential words and phrases that can be photocopied and given to children. As with the Hexagonie stories, these could be collated and made into a small booklet.

Vocabulary lists and materials needed

The vocabulary and materials needed are listed in boxes to the side of each section, so it is easy to see at a glance what vocabulary will be introduced, and what materials are needed. A full list of the vocabulary introduced in each unit is on pages 194–197.

Logos used in lesson plans

Each unit contains a wide variety of activities, ranging from role plays and games through to Mexican waves and listening activities. You do not need to do all the activities and you should use your professional judgement to decide which to include. Other suggestions for introducing vocabulary appear on page 9.

The following logos have been used to make the lesson plans easy to navigate:

 Role play is an excellent way of giving children the opportunity to practise speaking French.

 This logo is used to indicate that flashcards are to be used. Some flashcards appear on pages 224–227. You can easily make your own for other topics using pictures cut from magazines, downloaded from the internet or photocopied from the photocopiable sheets in this book. A set of colour flashcards can be purchased separately (ISBN 978 1 905780 60 0). A list of the flashcards included in this pack appears on page 217.

 This logo refers to the photocopiable pupil sheets. The number of the sheet is indicated on the logo. For more information on the pupil sheets, please see page 8.

 This logo indicates that a track on the CD is required. The appropriate track number appears on the logo.

 On the board – this logo indicates when it would be beneficial to illustrate the key points being taught on the board.

 Game – this logo is used to indicate a variety of games – some paper-based, others more active.

 Memory tricks are an important part of the *Hexagonie* approach. I provide a wide range of tried and tested "memory tricks" based on sound and idea associations. They enliven and facilitate the learning process by helping pupils to learn and remember what is being taught. Wherever memory tricks are used to master tricky grammatical points or vocabulary, experience shows that what is learnt once usually sticks for good. So, whenever a teacher or pupil faces a difficulty in French, the best solution is to use or devise a memory trick – what was difficult before will suddenly seem much easier and is less likely to be forgotten.

Throughout the scheme, pupils (and teachers!) are encouraged to construct their own memory tricks. Creating memory tricks is all about playing with words: it is an imaginative "game" which makes learning fun and also teaches pupils how to learn more efficiently. That means not just learning something for today, but knowing how to learn something so that you remember it for life.

Pupil pages

A variety of pupil pages has been included, so that you can choose the sheet most appropriate for your pupils. The pupil pages use the following logos, to help give pupils independence and instil confidence when reading instructions.

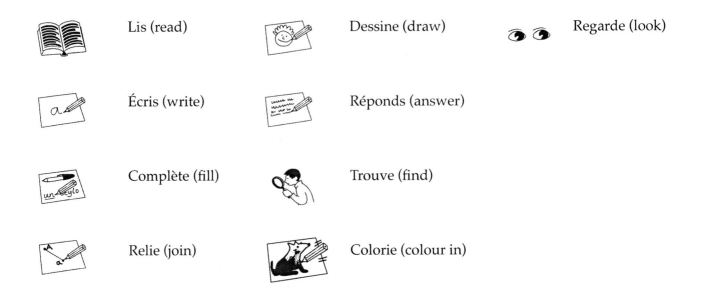

Lis (read)

Dessine (draw)

Regarde (look)

Écris (write)

Réponds (answer)

Complète (fill)

Trouve (find)

Relie (join)

Colorie (colour in)

Answers to the pupil sheets are given on pages 220–223.

Audio CD

The CD contains 41 tracks. A full transcript appears on pages 208–216. The oral activities on the CD model the language introduced in the scheme and provide listening activities, which gradually grow in length and complexity. Some of the listening activities are linked to specific worksheets. In addition there are four songs, as well as instrumental versions of the tunes to allow children to try singing on their own. After listening to the tracks, you could ask questions to test the pupils' comprehension and give them more opportunities for speaking.

Four characters are introduced in the CD tracks:
- Le Roi Être, King Être, the king of the imaginary land of Hexagonie
- Monsieur Grand (Mr Tall)
- Madame Petite (Mrs Short)
- Mademoiselle Jolie (Miss Pretty)

You could make stick puppets for these characters using the pictures on pages 204–207. Either you or your pupils could colour in the characters (photocopied onto card), then cut them out and glue lolly sticks to the back for handles. The puppets can then be used to practise conversations.

How Hexagonie relates to the KS2 Framework for Languages

Hexagonie, Part 1 addresses all of the learning objectives for Year 3 and 4 for Oracy and Literacy, and many of those for Intercultural Understanding. The charts below show which objectives are addressed in each unit. As you will see, most of the learning objectives are addressed in each Unit, so that pupils are given many opportunities to practise both their oral and written skills. Through doing the activities suggested in *Hexagonie*, pupils will also develop knowledge about the French language, and develop effective learning strategies for learning languages. Indeed, developing effective strategies for learning French is what *Hexagonie* is all about.

	O3.1	O3.2	O3.2	O3.3	O3.4	L3.1	L3.2	L3.3	IU3.1	IU3.2	IU3.3	IU3.4
1		•	•	•	•	•	•	•		•	*	**
2	•	•	•	•	•	•	•				*	**
3		•	•	•	•	•	•	•			•*	**
4		•	•	•	•	•	•	•			*	**
5	•	•	•	•	•	•					•*	**
6	•	•	•	•	•	•	•	•			*	**
7		•	•	•	•	•	•	•		•	*	**
8		•	•	•	•	•	•	•		•	*	**
9	•	•	•	•	•	•	•	•			*	**
10	•	•	•	•	•	•	•	•			*	**
11	•	•	•	•	•	•	•	•			*	**
12		•	•	•	•	•	•	•		•	•*	**
13		•	•	•	•	•	•	•		•	•*	**
14		•	•	•	•	•	•	•			•*	**
15		•	•	•	•	•	•	•			*	**

* *Greeting people politely is a very important part of French culture and throughout* Hexagonie *the importance of being polite and identifying to whom one is speaking is emphasized.*

** *The CD provides opportunities for pupils to hear French spoken and sung in a variety of contexts. Pupils would obviously benefit from having contact with native speakers, either in person or via video or the Internet.*

	O4.1	O4.2	O4.3	O4.4	L4.1	L4.2	L4.3	L4.4	IU4.1	IU4.2	IU4.3	IU4.4
1		•	•	•	•		•					•
2		•	•	•	•		•	•				
3		•		•	•		•	•				
4	•	•		•	•	•	•	•				
5		•	•	•	•	•		•				
6		•		•	•		•	•				
7		•		•	•	•		•				•
8		•	•	•	•		•	•				
9	•	•			•	•		•				
10	•	•		•	•	•	•	•				
11		•	•		•		•	•				
12		•		•	•	•		•				
13		•	•	•	•	•		•				•
14	•	•		•	•		•	•		•		
15	•	•		•	•	•	•	•		•		

Suggestions for introducing new vocabulary

Throughout *Hexagonie, Part 1*, the vocabulary is introduced using visual material: items from the classroom, miniatures and flashcards. The vocabulary is given as a suggestion and it is up to you, the teacher, to decide if you introduce it all.

Experience shows that pupils learn in different ways, which is why I have included a variety of learning styles – from 'engaging' activities (role play, games) through to oral and written activities. Using the vocabulary in many different ways will help pupils to remember it.

Hexagonie is primarily an oral approach to learning French. Photocopiable sheets are included to enable the children to practise what they have learned in class or at home. They contain a variety of activities ranging from drawing and matching activities through to reading and writing practice. It is intended that they should be given out only at the end of the lesson, and that you go over the language on the sheet first with the children. However, it is up to you, the teacher, to decide which sheets to give out and when, as you are the one who knows your pupils best. Remember, it is important for children to have lots of practice pronouncing words orally before seeing them in the written form.

Praising pupils

The more French your pupils hear using the language structures introduced in *Hexagonie*, the better. Here are some simple phrases using "c'est" you can use when praising children:

• C'est amusant!	It is funny!
• C'est beau!	It is beautiful!
• C'est intéressant!	It is interesting!
• C'est correct!	It is correct!
• C'est excellent!	It is excellent!
• C'est très bien!	It is very well done!
• Ce n'est pas difficile!	It isn't difficult!
• C'est magnifique!	It is magnificent!
• C'est simple!	It is simple!

Other useful French phrases

• Ce n'est pas clair!	It isn't clear!
• C'est dangereux!	It is dangerous!
• Ce n'est pas normal!	It isn't normal!
• C'est difficile!	It is difficult!
• C'est impossible!	It is impossible!
• C'est incorrect!	It is incorrect!
• C'est délicieux!	It is delicious!

The things around me

Key teaching points/vocabulary

Greetings
Classroom and household items
The indefinite article ("a")

Bonjour, je suis...
Hello, I am...

Say "Bonjour" to the whole class, and encourage the pupils to reply "Bonjour" in chorus.

Introduce yourself by saying, "Bonjour, je suis Madame/Monsieur/Mademoiselle (your name)." Address a single pupil asking him/her the simple question, "Et toi?" and encourage him/her to reply, for example, "Je suis Thomas," or "Je suis Jade." Go around the classroom asking the same question to each pupil in turn. They will soon realize that "et toi?" means, "and you?"

 Encourage the pupils to go around the class greeting others, for example:

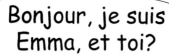

> **Bonjour, je suis Emma, et toi?**

> **Je suis Sunil.**

 1a Ask the pupils to complete Sheet 1a in the class or at home.

Note
We have not introduced "Je m'appelle..." at this stage because it is a complex verb that is better introduced later in the learning process. Also, "Je suis..." can serve as a key building block for a wide range of phrases and dialogues.

 Track 1 on the CD provides a listening activity to reinforce the vocabulary learned. It introduces Le Roi "Être", King Être, the king of the imaginary land of Hexagonie, and three other characters. You could make stick puppets using the pictures on pages 204–207 to act out this and other conversations between these characters.

Vocabulaire

bonjour	hello
je suis…	I am…
Madame	Mrs/Madam
Monsieur	Mr/Sir
Mademoiselle	Miss
et toi?	and you? (to a friend/child)
moi	me

Materials
★ Sheet 1a (page 16)
★ CD, Track 1

Vocabulaire

une porte	a door
une fenêtre	a window
une table	a table
une chaise	a chair
un stylo	a pen
un crayon	a pencil
une gomme	an eraser
une règle	a ruler
un cahier	a notebook
un papier	a piece of paper
une assiette	a plate
un couteau	a knife
une fourchette	a fork
une cuillère	a spoon
une bouteille	a bottle
une plante	a plant
très bien	well done
bravo	bravo
je suis désolé(e)	I am sorry
je ne sais pas	I don't know

Materials

★ Miniatures of household items (optional)
★ Flashcards for classroom objects and other words listed in Vocabulaire (optional)
★ "Je suis désolé(e)…" (page 198)
★ Sheets 1b and 1c (pages 17–18)
★ Sheets 1d(i)–1d(ii) (pages 19–20), photocopied back-to-back and cut into cards, one set per child/group
★ CD, Tracks 2 and 3
★ Scrap paper
★ Pencils for drawing

Un stylo, une table...
A pen, a table...

Point at and name an item in the classroom. For example, point at the door and say "une porte". Encourage the pupils to repeat the word in chorus.

Introduce more items in the same way, always with the pupils repeating the French word after you in chorus:

une fenêtre	une gomme	une chaise
un stylo	une règle	une table
un papier	un crayon	un cahier

Once the pupils are familiar with these items, start pointing at some of them without saying the French word, and wait for the pupils to say it for you.

When the pupils have grasped the names of classroom items, introduce the names of household items in a similar way, by pointing to miniatures or flashcards. I recommend using miniatures (e.g. doll's house furniture) as a practical and engaging way of extending the vocabulary being introduced beyond items found in the classroom. But if you do not have miniatures or other "props", you could use flashcards or draw pictures on the board.

Always praise a correct response with "Très bien, Emily", "Bravo, Henry!" in order to build your pupils' confidence.

If a pupil does not remember a French word, get them to let you know by reading out the sheet which says: "Je suis désolé(e), Madame/Monsieur, je ne sais pas." ("I am sorry Madam/Sir, I don't know.") (page 198) In the early stages, hold up this sheet every time a pupil gets stuck. After a while the pupils will know this useful phrase by heart and will automatically use it if needed.

Ask the pupils to complete Sheet 1b in the class or at home.

Using some of the vocabulary with which the pupils are now familiar, write two columns on the board, one containing masculine words (which take "un") and the other containing feminine words (which use "une"). In the column containing the feminine words, underline the "e" in "une" and the last "e" in the word itself:

un stylo	un<u>e</u> port<u>e</u>
un cahier	un<u>e</u> chais<u>e</u>
un crayon	un<u>e</u> tabl<u>e</u>
un papier	un<u>e</u> assiett<u>e</u>
un couteau	un<u>e</u> fourchett<u>e</u>

Explain to the pupils that "un" and "une" both mean "one" or "a". Since "une" ends in "e", it goes with most words ending in "e" (feminine words). "Un" goes with most words that do not end in "e" (masculine words).

Note
There are, of course, exceptions to this rule, and these will be introduced later on.

Ask the pupils to complete Sheet 1c in the class or at home.

For the listening activity on Track 2, each child will need a set of cards made from Sheets 1d(i) and 1d(ii). (Only the picture cards are required for this activity, but the words are needed on the back of the cards for the game below, so it is worth photocopying the sheets back-to-back at this stage.) The children listen to the words spoken on the CD and hold up the correct cards. The activity could also be done as a group activity.

For Track 3 each child will need a piece of scrap paper and a pencil. They will need to draw pictures of the words spoken on the CD. Encourage quick sketches.

Vocabulaire

un sandwich	a sandwich
une salade	a salad
une orange	an orange
une banane	a banana
un kiwi	a kiwi
un chocolat	a chocolate
un passeport	a passport
une visite	a visit
un train	a train
un poster	a poster
une lampe	a lamp
un miroir	a mirror
un pull-over	a pullover
un short	a pair of shorts
un pyjama	a pair of pyjamas

Materials

★ Sheets 1d(i)–1d(ii) (pages 19–20) photocopied back-to-back and cut into cards, two sets per group
★ Stickers (optional)

Mots similaires
Similar words

Write the words in the *Vocabulaire* list on the board, without "un" or "une". These words are ones which the pupils will recognize as being very similar or identical to English. Read out each word as you write it so that the pupils hear the French way of pronouncing them, which is different from English.

Ask the pupils to guess which of the words will be introduced by "un" and which will be introduced by "une". Get the pupils to sort the words into lists on a piece of paper, with all the words taking "un" in the left-hand column and all the words taking "une" in the right-hand column.

When they have finished this activity, congratulate the pupils saying, "Bravo!", "Très bien, Surinda!", "Très bien, Luke!" etc. Stickers are also always appreciated (see Resources , pages 218–219, for suppliers of French stickers).

Divide the pupils into groups of four to six and give each group two sets of the cards made from Sheets 1d(i) and 1d(ii). Ask them to place the cards in a pile in the middle of the table, with the picture-side facing up.

In turn each pupil picks up a card, looks at it and says the French word for the object shown if they know it. The pupil then checks if his/her word is correct by turning the card over. If it is correct, he/she keeps the card, but if it is incorrect, the card must be placed back at the bottom of the pile and the next child has a go.

If the pupil doesn't think he/she knows the French word, he/she says "Je suis désolé(e), je ne sais pas," turns the card over and reads out the French word. Then he/she puts the card back at the bottom of the pile.

The winner is the pupil who ends up with the most cards.

Hexagonie story

Ask the pupils to look at where France is on a map of Europe (Sheet 1e). Ask them to look closely at the shape of France and to say what shape it resembles (a hexagon). French people often use the word "l'hexagone" when referring to their own country.

Give every pupil a copy of Sheet 1f: "In Hexagonie". This introduces the imaginary land of Hexagonie, in which the French language comes alive to help pupils understand and speak it.

Read the sheet with your pupils and talk about male and female words in French. Make sure the pupils know what a noun is. You could say that a noun is a naming word like "un papier, une chaise". Point out that in French the word "nom" means "name" and "noun". There will be other Hexagonie stories in each of the following units.

Materials
★ Sheet 1e and 1f (pages 21–22)

Essential words and phrases

At the end of the unit, give the pupils Sheet 1g to help them remember some essential words and phrases.

Materials
★ Sheet 1g (page 23)

Au revoir!
Goodbye!

Finish the lesson by saying "Au revoir" and by waving or shaking every pupil's hand. Expect them to reply, "Au revoir" in chorus or individually.

Vocabulaire

au revoir   goodbye

Nom:_____ **La date:**_____

Regarde et lis

Look and read

Bonjour, je suis Florian, et toi?

Bonjour, moi, je suis Michelle.

Dessine et écris

Draw (or stick) a picture of yourself in the frame, and write in French, "Hello, I am (your name)."

_____

_____

Moi (me)

Nom:_____ **La date:**_____

Regarde 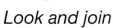 et relie

Look and join

1. une plante

2. un stylo

3. une fourchette

4. une chaise

5. une bouteille

6. un cahier

7. une gomme

8. une règle

9. une fenêtre

10. un couteau

11. une assiette

12. une cuillère

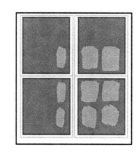

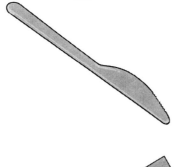

Regarde 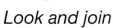 et relie

© Maria Rice-Jones and Brilliant Publications

Nom:_____   **La date:**_____

Ecris

Write "un" or "une" in front of each word.

1. ____ assiett**e**   2. ____ plant**e**   3. ____ couteau

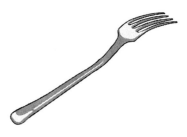      

4. ____ fourchett**e**   5. ____ cuillèr**e**   6. ____ port**e**

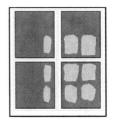      

7. ____ fenêtr**e**   8. ____ cahier   9. ____ crayon

   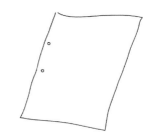   

10. ____ stylo   11. ____ papier   12. ____ gomm**e**

13. ____ règl**e**   14. ____ bouteill**e**   15. ____ tabl**e**

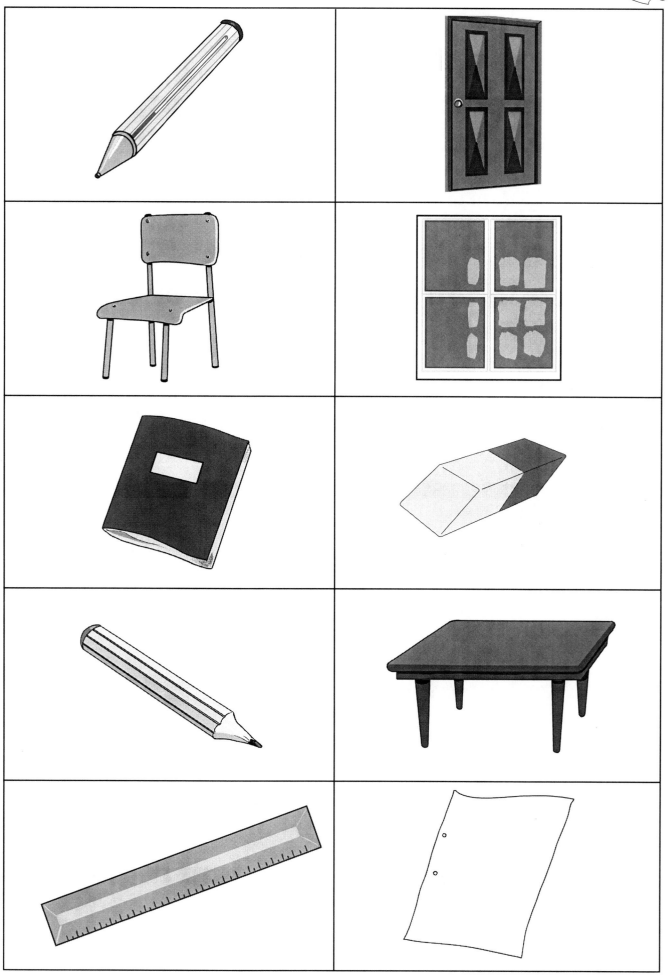

Hexagonie, Part 1 19
© Maria Rice-Jones and Brilliant Publications

une porte	**un stylo**
une fenêtre	**une chaise**
une gomme	**un cahier**
une table	**un crayon**
un papier	**une règle**

Nom:_____   **La date:**_____

Regarde 👀

Look at the map of Europe.

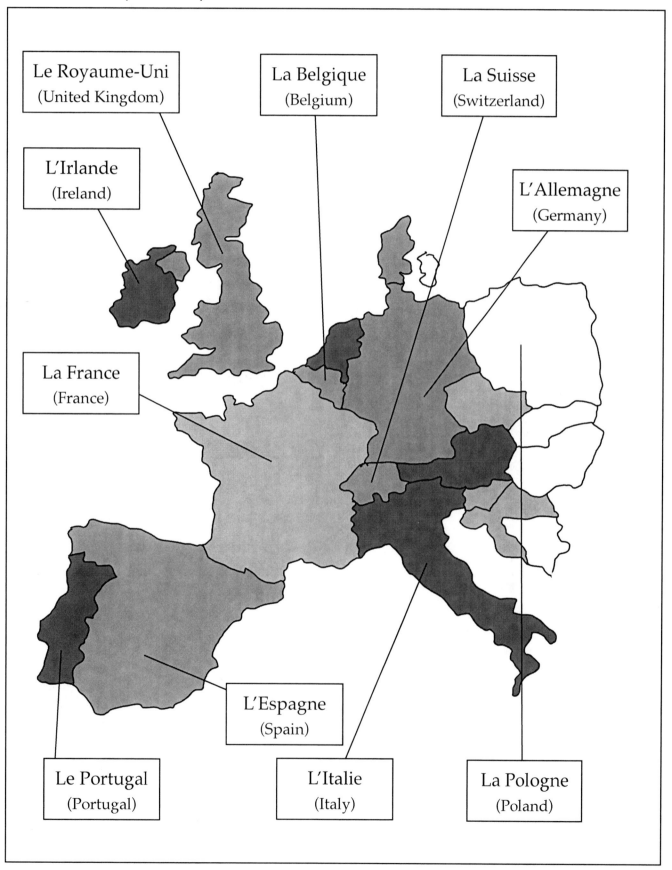

Nom:_____   **La date:**_____

In Hexagonie

Once upon a time there was a country whose shape looked so much like a hexagon that everyone living there decided to give it the unusual name of "Hexagonie".

The inhabitants of Hexagonie belonged to different groups and each group had a specific job to do. One of the biggest groups was known as the nouns. Their job was naming all the different things in the land.

As soon as they were born, all nouns had to be registered. Females were given names ending in "e", while the males had names ending in letters other than "e".

So, for example, the noun  was female,

but the noun _crayon_ was male.

All the female nouns had a special playmate called "une". They always followed her around whenever they were alone. They liked their little playmate because she ended in the letter "e" just like they did! All over Hexagonie, you could see thousands of "une" playmates followed by their female nouns.

The male nouns had a playmate too – but their playmate was called "un". They did not want a playmate ending in "e" like the girls! All over the land you could see thousands of little "un" playmates followed by their male nouns.

Nom:_____ **La date:**_____

Essential words and phrases

How to greet people

Bonjour, Madame	Hello, Madam
Bonjour, Monsieur	Hello, Sir
Bonjour, Mademoiselle	Hello, Miss

Note

French people like to show who they are talking to in order to be polite. If you don't do it, it is often seen as rude.

How to say you don't know

Je suis désolé(e), Madame/ Monsieur, je ne sais pas.	I am sorry, Madam/Sir, I don't know.

Note

When a boy writes this sentence, he must write "désolé", but when a girl writes the same sentence, she must write "désolée" with an extra "e" at the end of the word – just like the female nouns in Hexagonie!

How to ask the teacher to repeat something

Répétez, Madame/ Monsieur, s'il vous plaît.	Please Madame/Sir, would you repeat that?

Saying goodbye

Au revoir	Goodbye (This really means "till we see each other again")

Unit 2

How to introduce things

Key teaching points/vocabulary

The alphabet
Simple sentences with "c'est" ("it is")
Clothing

Vocabulaire

ça va bien?	how are things?
ça va bien, merci	everything's fine, thank you
merci	thank you
l'appel (m)	the register
présent(e)	present
absent(e)	absent

Materials

★ CD, Track 4

Bonjour, ça va bien?

Hello, how are things?

Say "Bonjour" to the whole class waiting for the pupils to reply. "Bonjour, Madame/Monsieur."

Call the register ("l'appel"), expecting the pupils to respond "présent(e)" when their name is called out. If there is no answer say "absent(e)".

Note
During the following lessons, when you call the register expect every pupil to respond "présent(e)" when their name is called out. As this word is similar in English, the pupils will easily remember it.

Tell the pupils that at the beginning of every lesson you will ask some pupils how they are by saying, "Ça va bien?", which means "How are things?" Tell the pupils that they have to answer, "Ça va bien, merci," which means, "Everything's fine, thank you." Then call out the name of a pupil and ask him/her, "Ça va bien, Joshua/ Marie?", waiting for the pupil to reply, "Ça va bien, merci." Then ask the next child, "Et toi, (name of child), ça va bien?"

Notes
The cedilla under the "c" in "ça va" changes the sound to a soft "c" ("s" sound), as in "centre" in English.

In Unit 5 the more personal greeting "Comment vas-tu?" is introduced.

In the listening activity on Track 4, le Roi Être greets Monsieur Grand, Madame Petite and Mademoiselle Jolie. You could act out the conversation using stick puppets made from the pictures on pages 204–207.

Note
"Toi" is the form of "you" used when talking to children and/or close friends. The king, being much more important than the others, uses "toi" to talk to his subjects.

Ask for volunteers to perform a similar dialogue, imagining that one pupil meets another one in the street and greets him/her by saying:

> Bonjour, Shaun!

> Bonjour, Gabriella! Ça va bien?

> Ça va bien merci, et toi?

> Moi, ça va bien.

Recap on vocabulary for classroom and household items

Point at an item in the class introduced in Unit 1 (e.g. a door) and wait for all the pupils to say the French word ("une porte"). Do the same with more items, using flashcards and miniatures if necessary, until you feel the pupils can remember most of them.

Materials

★ Flashcards of classroom objects
★ Miniatures (optional)

L'alphabet

The alphabet

Vocabulaire

oui	yes
non	no

Materials

★ CD, Tracks 5–7
★ Tableau d'Honneur (page 203)

Write the letter "a" on the board and say the sound "a" in French, waiting for the pupils to repeat the sound in chorus after you. Continue with all the letters of the alphabet. At this stage introduce letters without accents only.

Sing the alphabet to the tune of "Twinkle, twinkle little star" and encourage the whole class to join in with you. On Track 5 the song is sung all the way through. On Tracks 6 and 7 some letters are missing. The pupils will need to try to fill in the missing letters as they sing along.

Notes
If you don't use the CD you will need to modify the ending of "Twinkle, twinkle little star" slightly to get the alphabet to fit the tune.

The last two lines of the song are as follows:

Voilà je sais mon abc	There! I know my abc
Alors c'est à toi maintenant.	Now it's your turn.

Divide the pupils into groups of four to six and ask each group to sing in front of the class. Decide which group has sung best and reward every member of that group with a "Tableau d'Honneur" (a Merit Certificate, see page 203).

Write on the board the names of some pupils or some famous people (e.g. David Beckham and Thierry Henry). Ask the pupils to perform a Mexican wave where the first pupil will say the first letter of the name in French, the second pupil will say the second letter and so on.

Play "Le pendu" (hangman) using the names or surnames of the pupils in the class. The pupils must say the letter names in French. Use "oui" or "non" to say whether a letter is correct or not.

Materials

★ Sheet 2a (page 29)

Hexagonie story

Give the pupils Sheet 2a: "The army of letters", which is the next instalment in the Hexagonie story. Read this with the pupils and then recap on the song as a class.

Vocabulaire

c'est   it is/it's
c'est correct   it's correct

Materials

★ Flashcards of classroom objects
★ Sheet 2b (page 30)

C'est un cahier

It's a notebook

Go around the classroom, point at a window and say, "C'est une fenêtre," then at a notebook and say, "C'est un cahier," and so on until you have said at least ten well-known items.

Ask the pupils if they have understood what "c'est" means. Tell them that "c'est" means "it is" (or "it's").

Point at the door and ask the entire class, "C'est une porte?" waiting for the pupils to answer in chorus, "Oui, c'est une porte."

Give a lot of praise: "Très bien!", "Bravo!", "Oui, c'est correct, bravo!"

Point to other classroom items introduced in Unit 1 and ask the same type of question. Make sure each question requires a positive answer. You could use flashcards instead.

Then ask questions which present the pupils with two options. For example, hold up the flashcard showing a table and ask, "C'est une table ou une chaise?", waiting for the pupils to answer "C'est une table."

Ask the pupils to draw the things indicated on Sheet 2b either in class or at home.

C'est une jupe; c'est un pantalon

It's a skirt; it's a pair of trousers

Point at an item of clothing or flashcard (e.g. a skirt) and say, "C'est une jupe," encouraging the pupils to repeat it. Then introduce a second item of clothing or flashcard (e.g. a hat) and say, "C'est un chapeau," asking the pupils to repeat it. Then repeat the first and the second item again and encourage all the pupils to repeat them. Then introduce the third item in the same way. Once the pupils are familiar with all the articles of clothing, point at an item of clothing or a flashcard and wait for the pupils to say the French word for you.

Hold up a flashcard or item of clothing. First say the French word and then spell it. Ask the pupils to write the letters as you say them, and when they have written down the word letter by letter, ask them to spell it back to you.

Divide the pupils into pairs. Give every pupil a set of cards made from Sheets 2c(i) and 2c(ii). The first player must show the picture side of all ten cards one by one to his/her partner, who must call out the French word for the item on each card in less than five seconds, e.g. "C'est un manteau," "C'est une cravate," etc. When the ten cards have all been shown tell the pupil who was shown the cards to add up his/her score, then swap roles and play again. The winner is the pupil who has said the most French words correctly.

On Sheet 2d the pupils will need to write "un" or "une" in front of the words indicated.

Essential words and phrases

At the end of this unit, give the pupils Sheet 2e, which will help them to remember essential words or phrases.

Vocabulaire

un pantalon	a pair of trousers
une jupe	a skirt
un pull-over	a jumper
une chemise	a shirt
un manteau	a coat
une veste	a jacket
un short	a pair of shorts
une ceinture	a belt
un chapeau	a hat
une cravate	a tie
un pyjama	a pair of pyjamas
une robe	a dress

Materials

★ Items of clothing
★ Flashcards of items of clothing
★ Sheets 2c(i)–2c(ii) (pages 31–32) photocopied back-to-back and cut into cards, one set per pupil
★ Sheet 2d (page 33)

Materials

★ Sheet 2e (page 34)

Vocabulaire

bonne	have a good
semaine	week
vous aussi	you too

Au revoir! Bonne semaine!

Goodbye! Have a good week!

Say "Au revoir!" to your pupils and when you shake their hands tell them that you are going to wish them a good week by saying, "Bonne semaine!" Ask them to reply, "Vous aussi!"

Note

"Tu" is used for speaking to one person and only for friends, relatives and children. "Vous" is used instead of "tu" for talking to a person you don't know very well or to a person who is older than you as a sign of respect. It is also used for talking to a group of people.

Nom:_____ **La date:**_____

The army of letters

In Hexagonie, there lived an army of 26 letters whose job was to build words. With so many words, they had a very busy life and most letters had little or no time to sleep. They enjoyed their job though, as they knew that without them, there would not be any words at all!

Every morning the letters would line up and parade in front of the Hexagonian royal family. Each letter in turn would march across the parade yard singing out who they were. This reminded everyone how important the letters were.

You can sing along with the letters, because they sang their song to the tune, "Twinkle, twinkle little star".

© Maria Rice-Jones and Brilliant Publications

Nom:_____   **La date:**_____

Lis [✎] et dessine

Read and draw

1. C'est une porte.	2. C'est une chaise.
3. C'est une gomme.	4. C'est une assiette.
5. C'est un couteau.	6. C'est un crayon.
7. C'est une bouteille.	8. C'est un cahier.

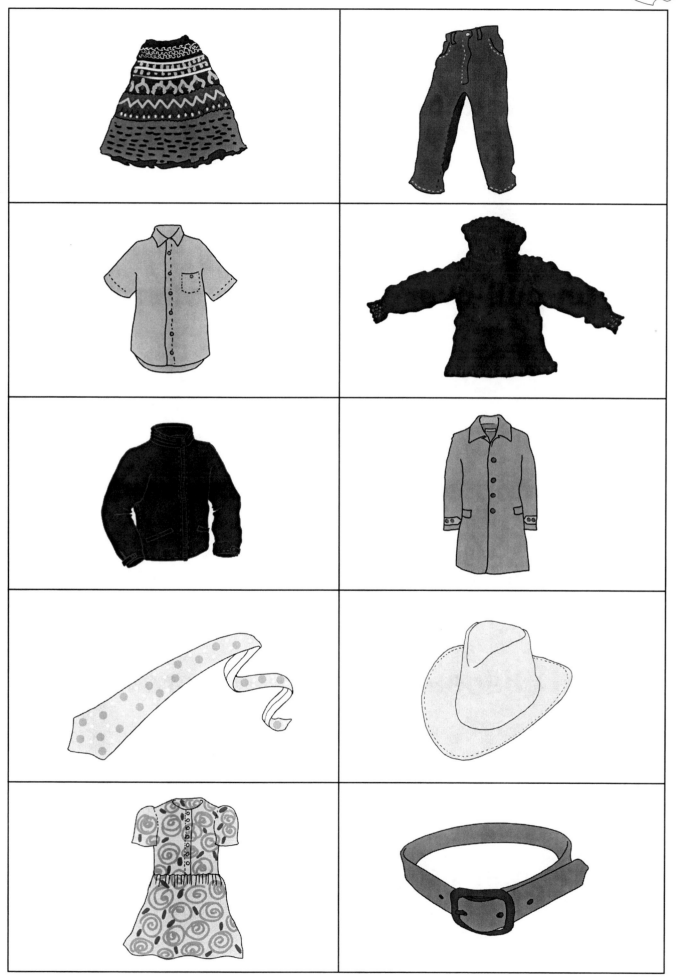

© Maria Rice-Jones and Brilliant Publications

un pantalon	**une jupe**
un pull-over	**une chemise**
un manteau	**une veste**
un chapeau	**une cravate**
une ceinture	**une robe**

Nom:_____ **La date:**_____

Écris

Write "un" or "une" in each sentence.

1. C'est _____ pantalon. 2. C'est _____ jup**e**. 3. C'est _____ pyjama.

4. C'est _____ vest**e**. 5. C'est _____ chemis**e**. 6. C'est _____ chapeau.

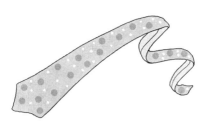

7. C'est _____ pull-over. 8. C'est _____ cravat**e**. 9. C'est _____ rob**e**.

10. C'est _____ manteau. 11. C'est _____ ceintur**e**. 12. C'est _____ short.

© Maria Rice-Jones and Brilliant Publications

Nom:_____   **La date:**_____

Essential words and phrases

How to thank somebody

Merci	Thank you
Merci Madame	Thank you Madam
Merci Monsieur	Thank you Sir
Merci Mademoiselle	Thank you Miss

How to say "It's correct; it's very good"

C'est correct.	It's correct.
C'est très bien.	It's very good.

How to talk about how someone is

Ça va?	How are things?
Ça va bien, merci.	Everything's fine, thank you.

How to say "yes" and "no"

Oui	Yes
Non	No

How to reply when your teacher wishes you a good week ("Bonne semaine")

Vous aussi	You too

The colours of the rainbow

Key teaching points/vocabulary

Colours
Negative form "ce n'est pas" ("it isn't")
Bedroom furniture

Bonjour/l'appel

Hello/the register

Say "Bonjour" to the whole class, waiting for the pupils to reply, "Bonjour Madame/Monsieur." If pupils are standing, ask them to sit down by miming this action and by saying "Asseyez-vous, s'il vous plaît." For more classroom commands see pages 201–202.

Call the register, saying if the pupil called is "présent(e)" or "absent(e)". Ask the children how they are by using "Ça va bien?"

Vocabulaire

Asseyez-vous, s'il vous plaît!   Sit down, please! (to a group)

Materials

★ Useful classroom commands (pages 201–202)

Recap on "c'est"

Hold up a classroom object that you are sure the children know the French word for. Ask, for example, "C'est un stylo?" and wait for them to reply, "Oui, c'est un stylo." Repeat with a number of items so that the pupils can practise "c'est". Stick to positive answers only.

Vocabulaire

ce n'est pas correct   it's not correct

Materials

★ Items of clothing
★ Flashcards of items of clothing, e.g. made from Sheet 2c(i) (page 31)

 Using the clothes flashcards (or actual items of clothing), move on to asking the whole class questions such as "C'est une jupe ou une veste?"

Congratulate a correct answer with an enthusiastic "Bravo, c'est très bien!"

When an answer is incorrect, shake your head and say, "Je suis désolé(e), ce n'est pas correct." This will help the pupils to gradually become familiar with the negative "ce n'est pas", which is introduced later in the unit.

 Give ten pupils one clothes flashcard each. Point at one pupil's flashcard (let's imagine it is of a shirt) and ask him/her, "C'est une chemise?" Wait for the pupil to answer, "Oui, c'est une chemise." Then encourage another pupil to ask a similar question to a pupil of his/her choice, for example, "C'est un pantalon?" if the flashcard is of a pair of trousers. Continue going around the class in this way. Swap to allow everyone to have a chance to ask and answer questions.

Vocabulaire

bleu(e)	blue
brun(e)	brown
orange	orange
noir(e)	black
rouge	red
jaune	yellow
rose	pink
vert(e)	green
gris(e)	grey
blanc(he)	white

Materials

★ Sheets 3a and 3b (pages 40–41)

Les couleurs

The colours

The colours blue, brown and orange in English sound almost the same in French: "bleu(e)", "brun(e)" and "orange". It is therefore helpful to introduce these colours first before moving on to the others.

Point at an item in the classroom and ask a question giving the pupils the choice between two different colours, "C'est un pantalon bleu ou c'est un pantalon orange?" Wait for the pupils to reply in chorus, "C'est un pantalon bleu." For now, only use masculine nouns, e.g. un pantalon, un pull-over, un chapeau, un stylo, un papier, un cahier, etc.

Point at other items in the room and ask the same type of question mentioning two colours. One of the two colours should always be blue so that the pupils understand by deduction which answer is right, e.g. pointing at a red pen ask, "C'est un stylo bleu ou rouge?" and wait for the answer, "C'est un stylo rouge." Tell the pupils that in French, contrary to in English, the adjective follows the noun.

Bleu ou bleue?

Blue (m) or blue (f)?

Some colour words sound the same whether they are in the masculine or the feminine so it is easiest to introduce these first. Point to objects in the room to practise these colours, asking questions such as, "C'est un crayon jaune ou un crayon rouge?"

bleu	bleue
noir	noire
orange	orange
rouge	rouge
jaune	jaune
rose	rose

Then practise the colours which do not sound the same in the masculine and in the feminine:

vert	verte
brun	brune
gris	grise
blanc	blanche

Congratulate the pupils with, "Bravo, c'est correct."

When you are confident that the pupils know the way the words sound, show them how the spellings differ between the masculine and feminine forms by writing the words on the board.

Ask pupils to complete Sheet 3a either in the class or at home. On this sheet the children need to read the sentences and draw an appropriately coloured object.

You can use Sheet 3b to help children become familiar with the spellings of colour words in both the masculine and feminine form.

Hexagonie story

Give the pupils Sheet 3c: "The colourful kingdom". Discuss to reinforce the points covered.

Materials
★ Sheet 3c (page 42)

Forme négative "ce n'est pas"

Negative form "ce n'est pas"

Take a notebook in one hand, point at it, shaking your head, and say: "Ce n'est pas un stylo. Ce n'est pas un papier. Ce n'est pas un passeport. Ce n'est pas un crayon, mais (say "but") c'est un cahier."

Point at a pen asking the whole class, "C'est un crayon?" and wait for the pupils to answer in chorus, "Non, ce n'est pas un crayon." Do not let them say what it is, as the purpose of this activity is to practise "ce n'est pas".

Then ask, "C'est une bouteille?" and wait for the pupils to answer in chorus, "Non, ce n'est pas une bouteille." Continue asking questions which require a negative answer with "ce n'est pas" and finally pretending to be exasperated ask, "Qu'est-ce que c'est?" At last the pupils will be very pleased to let you know that, "C'est un stylo."

Vocabulaire

ce n'est pas   it isn't
mais   but
Qu'est-ce que   What is it?
c'est?

Materials
★ CD, Track 8
★ Sheet 2c(i) (page 31), one per pupil. Before photocopying, number the pictures as follows: 1 skirt, 2 pair of trousers, 3 shirt, 4 jumper, 5 jacket, 6 coat, 7 tie, 8 hat, 9 dress, 10 belt

Divide the pupils into pairs. Ask them to put at least five classroom objects on the table. The pupils take it in turns to ask each other questions about the objects, for example, "C'est un stylo?" and his/her partner must answer, "Oui, c'est un stylo," or "Non, ce n'est pas un stylo, mais c'est un crayon."

Each pupil will need a copy of Sheet 2c(i) (see Materials) when listening to Track 8 on the CD. Encourage the children to answer the questions during the pauses on the CD, using "c'est" and "ce n'est pas".

Vocabulaire

un lit	a bed
une armoire	a wardrobe
une commode	a chest of drawers
un bureau	a desk
un divan	a sofa
un fauteuil	an armchair
un coussin	a cushion
un ordinateur	a computer
une lampe	a lamp
un miroir	a mirror
un tableau	a painting
une horloge	a clock

Materials

★ Flashcards of items of furniture found in the bedroom
★ Miniatures of bedroom furniture (e.g. doll's house furniture)
★ Bag or box
★ Sheets 3d and 3e (pages 43–44)
★ Coloured pencils

Materials

★ Sheet 3f (page 45)

Dans la chambre

In the bedroom

Use flashcards or miniatures of bedroom furniture. Point at an item (let's imagine it is of an armchair) and say, "C'est un fauteuil," encouraging the pupils to repeat it. Then introduce a second item (a bed) and say, "C'est un lit," asking the pupils to repeat it. Then repeat both items and encourage all the pupils to repeat them. Then introduce the remaining items in the same way. Once the pupils are familiar with most of the words, point at an item without saying the French word and wait for the pupils to say it for you.

Hide one of the flashcards or miniatures in a bag (or box) and encourage all the pupils to guess what the item is, e.g. "C'est un miroir?" Answer with a complete sentence, "Non, ce n'est pas un miroir," to reinforce the negative "ce n'est pas." You could give them a certain number of guesses. If they don't guess it correctly then say, "Ce n'est pas un tableau mais c'est un lit." Do the same with some more items. You can make this game harder or easier by varying the number of items.

3d

Ask the pupils to colour the items on Sheet 3d using six different colours of their choice. Encourage them to write under each item, "C'est une lampe verte," etc. This sheet also reinforces the use of "un" and "une".

3e

Ask the pupils to complete Sheet 3e, answering the questions with "ce n'est pas…" As the pupils will not have seen "ce n'est pas" in the written form, it is important to go over the sheet with them first. Fast finishers could be asked to answer the questions with the correct noun, either orally (in pairs) or in writing.

Essential words and phrases

3f

At the end of this unit, give the pupils Sheet 3f, which will help them to remember essential words and phrases.

Au revoir! Bonne journée! Bon week-end!

Vocabulaire

Bonne journée!   Have a good day!

Bon week-end!   Have a good weekend!

Materials

★ CD, Track 9

Goodbye! Have a good day! Have a good weekend!

Remember always to wish the pupils a good day or weekend, depending on when the lesson takes place. Wait for them to reply, "Merci, Madame/Monsieur, vous aussi."

Let the pupils listen to Track 9, where le Roi Être and the other characters say goodbye to each other.

Note

In French culture, it is considered very rude not to greet people and say goodbye politely. For this reason you should start every lesson with "Bonjour" and end with "Au revoir" In both instances insist that the pupils reply politely, saying "Bonjour, Madame/Monsieur" and "Merci, Madame/Monsieur, vous aussi."

Nom:_____   **La date:**_____

Lis 📖 et dessine ✏️

Read and draw

1. C'est une cuillère verte.	2. C'est un chapeau rouge.
3. C'est une robe rose.	4. C'est une table brune.
5. C'est un pantalon noir.	6. C'est un pull-over orange.
7. C'est une fourchette grise.	8. C'est un short jaune.

Nom:_____ **La date:**_____

A. Complète

Fill in the blanks as in the example.

	un pyjama	**une chemise**
Example	bleu	bleu<u>e</u>
	noir	noir_
	vert	vert_
	brun	brun_
	gris	gris_
	jaune	jaun_
	rouge	roug_
	rose	ros_
	orange	orang_

Attention!

un pyjama blanc   une chemise blan<u>**he**</u>

B. Écris

Write the names of colours which are written in the same way for both male and female nouns.

C. Écris

Write the names of colours which sound the same for "un" and "une".

© Maria Rice-Jones and Brilliant Publications

Nom:＿＿＿＿＿＿＿＿＿＿＿＿＿＿＿＿＿＿＿ **La date:**＿＿＿＿＿＿＿＿＿＿＿

The colourful kingdom

Hexagonie was a really colourful kingdom because its nouns went about dressed in different colours. Every noun wanted to be seen wearing the right colours for each season: bright colours for the summer and dark colours in the winter. The choice of colours was infinite, and with time Hexagonie became very well known for its fashion and elegance.

Male nouns looked nice in many colours, such as: "bleu", "brun", and "jaune".

However, the female nouns wanted to look more special than the male nouns, and they tried to find a way to attract more attention. They decided to wear the same colours but with something extra to make them look more feminine. So they added an "e" to their coloured clothes as well. Now all female colours ended in "e" and the female nouns felt very special because wherever they went, they were looked at.

A few female colours like "bleue" and "noire" did still sound the same as the male ones. But the female nouns didn't mind, because what really mattered was that they looked different thanks to their extra "e" – their favourite letter!

The female nouns loved wearing all different sorts of colours, but one colour was more special than all the others. This was the colour they wore on their wedding day – white. It was so special that they wanted to make it stand out even more. So, the female nouns decided to add another letter before the "e" and that is how the female colour "blanche" was born.

Nom:_____   **La date:**_____

Colorie et complète

Colour in the pictures and fill in the blanks. In the first blank write "un" or "une" and in the second blank write the French word for the colour you have chosen.

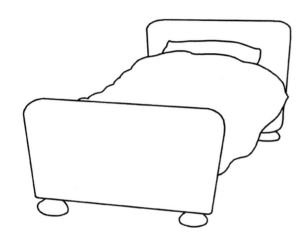

e.g. C'est <u>un</u> lit <u>bleu</u>.

1.   C'est _____ armoire _____.

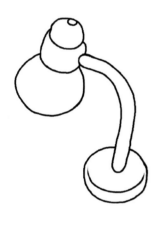

2.   C'est _____ lampe _____.

3.   C'est _____ fauteuil _____.

4.   C'est _____ commode _____.

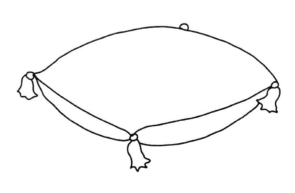

5.   C'est _____ coussin _____.

Nom:_____   **La date:**_____

Réponds

Answer these questions using "ce n'est pas…." The first one has been done for you.

e.g.   C'est un papier?

Non, ce n'est pas un papier. C'est une porte.

1.   C'est une plante?

_____

2.   C'est une table?

_____

3.   C'est un bureau?

_____

4.   C'est un ordinateur?

_____

5.   C'est un divan?

_____

Nom:_____ **La date:**_____

Essential words and phrases

How to thank somebody

Merci!	Thank you!
Merci Madame!	Thank you Madam!
Merci Monsieur!	Thank you Sir!
Merci Mademoiselle!	Thank you Miss!

How the teacher asks the class to sit down

Asseyez-vous, s'il vous plaît!   Sit down, please!

How to say "but"

mais   but

How to say "it is not"

ce n'est pas…   it is not…

How to reply when someone wishes you "Bonne semaine!" ("Have a good week!")

Vous aussi!   You too!

Note

"Vous aussi!" can also be used when replying to "Bonne journée!" ("Have a nice day!") or "Bon week-end!" ("Have a nice weekend!").

Unit 4

Be curious about things!

Key teaching points/vocabulary

Numbers 0–10
Days of the week
"Qu'est-ce que c'est?" ("What is it?")
"C'est combien?" ("How much is it?")

Bonjour/l'appel

Hello/the register

Say "Bonjour" to the whole class waiting for the pupils to reply, "Bonjour, Madame/Monsieur." Call the register, asking the children "Ça va bien?" as explained at the start of Units 2 and 3.

Recap on "c'est" and "ce n'est pas"

Point at an item and ask a pupil, "C'est une chaise verte?" and wait for a positive or a negative answer. Ask a pupil to point at an item and ask the same type of question to another pupil of his/her choice.

Vocabulaire

zéro	zero
un	one
deux	two
trois	three
quatre	four
cinq	five
six	six
sept	seven
huit	eight
neuf	nine
dix	ten

Materials

★ Small bag
★ Cards with numbers 0–10 in figures
★ Sheet 4a (page 51)
★ CD, Track 10

Nombres 0–10

Numbers 0–10

Count to three with your fingers, "un, deux, trois." Encourage the pupils to repeat these three numbers in chorus after you. Then continue with numbers up to 10.

 Write the numbers 0–10 on the board, one at a time. Encourage the class to call out each number in French after you write it.

Always congratulate a correct answer with an enthusiastic, "Très bien" or "Bravo".

Ask individual pupils to count from 0 to 10. If you think they are able, also ask them to count backwards from 10 to 0.

 Pupils pass round a bag containing cards with the numbers 0–10 on them in figures. When it is their turn, pupils pull out a card at random and say the number in French, after which they put the card back and pass the bag to the next player.

4a

Ask the pupils to complete Sheet 4a in the class or at home.

Track 10 will help the pupils to learn their numbers from 0–10. In the second part of the track they will be given a series of numbers and will have to work out the missing numbers.

Les jours de la semaine

The days of the week

Say that you are going to introduce the days of the week. Say one day at a time, encouraging the class to repeat each day after you, starting with "lundi".

Explain that in French each day from Monday to Friday takes its name from a different planet (heavenly body):

English	*French*	*Reason for name*
Monday	lundi	from the French word "lune" (moon)
Tuesday	mardi	from "Mars" (Mars)
Wednesday	mercredi	from "Mercure" (Mercury)
Thursday	jeudi	from "Jupiter" (Jupiter)
Friday	vendredi	from "Vénus" (Venus)

Call out the days in sequence, missing out one day and ask the pupils to tell you which day has been omitted. Ask individual pupils (at least five) to call out the days of the week starting with "lundi".

Perform a Mexican wave in which each pupil must say the next day, starting with "lundi", e.g. Harriet: "lundi", Rob: "mardi", Joshan: "mercredi", etc.

Say "aujourd'hui, today" three times and ask, "Aujourd'hui, c'est lundi?" and wait for the pupils to answer in chorus with "Oui, c'est lundi" or "Non, ce n'est pas lundi mais c'est mardi."

Write other days at random on the board and practise the same type of question and answer.

Call out the days at random in French. After each day, ask the pupils to write what it means in English on a card or piece of paper and then hold it up. Congratulate with an enthusiastic "très bien" or "parfait".

You will need to have several Cootie Catchers (sometimes called a "fortune teller" or a "Chinese counter") made from Sheet 4a. You could give the pupils a copy of the sheet and ask them to make one to bring to the next class.

Vocabulaire

lundi	Monday
mardi	Tuesday
mercredi	Wednesday
jeudi	Thursday
vendredi	Friday
samedi	Saturday
dimanche	Sunday
le week-end	the weekend
aujourd'hui	today

Materials

★ Sheet 4b (page 52) made into "Cootie Catchers" in advance either by you or the pupils
★ Sheet 4c (page 53)
★ CD, Tracks 11 and 12
★ Blank cards or spare pieces of paper

Divide the pupils into pairs. Pupils take turns at being the Cootie Master who holds the Cootie Catcher and starts the game by asking the other player to pick a number. The Cootie Master then opens and closes the Cootie Catcher that number of times while counting out aloud, "un, deux, trois" etc. When the Cootie Master has stopped counting, the other player must look inside the Cootie Catcher and choose one of the days that are shown. Then the Cootie Master must count how many letters that day contains and open and close the Cootie Catcher that number of times (so they would open and close it six times if the day was "samedi", for example). Once the Cootie Master has stopped counting (in French!), the player must look at the inside of the Cootie Catcher again and choose a day. The Cootie Master then flips up the panel with the chosen day on it, and reads out the question to their partner who has to answer by saying the correct day(s) in French.

Ask the pupils to complete the three activities on the days of the week on Sheet 4c in the class or at home.

Tracks 11 and 12 provide practice with the days of the week. On Track 11 pupils have to choose between two days. Track 12 is more difficult and should be used when the pupils are more confident, as the answer is not always given in the question. Encourage the pupils to respond in full sentences during the pauses.

Vocabulaire

un plafond	a ceiling
un sac	a bag
un mur	a wall
un bureau	a desk
un ordinateur	a computer
un poster	a poster
un tableau	a (black)board (or a painting)
un(e) élève	a pupil
un professeur	a teacher

Materials

★ Sheet 4d (page 54)

Qu'est-ce que c'est?

What is it?

Go around the classroom, point at different items known by the pupils and for each one ask the entire class, "Qu'est-ce que c'est?" The pupils will say in chorus, "C'est (name of the object)."

Now ask the same type of questions to the pupils individually. When the pupil knows what the object is, he/she must say, "C'est (object's name)", and when the pupil does not know what the object is, he/she must say "Je suis désolé(e) Madame/Monsieur, je ne sais pas." Encourage him/her to ask another pupil e.g. "Qu'est-ce que c'est, Rebecca?" waiting for her to say what the item is.

Encourage the pupils to point to different things in the room and ask you, "Qu'est-ce que c'est Madame/Monsieur?" This is a good opportunity for you to introduce new words such as "un plafond" (a ceiling), "un sac" (a bag), "un mur" (a wall), etc. See *Vocabulaire* for a list of useful words. If you don't know the word, don't be afraid to say "Je suis désolé(e), je ne sais pas."

When you say what it is, encourage the pupils to thank you individually by saying, "Merci Madame/Monsieur."

 Ask the pupils to complete Sheet 4d on "Qu'est-ce que c'est?" As the pupils will not have seen "Qu'est-ce que c'est?" in the written form, it is important to go over the sheet with them first.

Hexagonie story

 Give the pupils Sheet 4e: "It is good to be the king!", the next instalment in the Hexagonie story. Discuss to reinforce the points covered.

Materials
★ Sheet 4e (page 55)

Dans une boutique

In a clothes shop

Track 13 on the CD is a dialogue between a shop assistant in a clothes shop and a customer. The text appears in cartoon form on Sheet 4f so that the pupils may read along as they listen to it.

Divide the pupils into pairs. Give each pupil cards made from sheets 2c(i) and 2c(ii). One pupil will be the shop assistant and the other will be the customer. The shop assistant picks six cards with the pictures of items of clothes he/she wants to sell, and then sets them out on the table. The shop assistant then greets the customer who asks, "Qu'est-ce que c'est, s'il vous plaît?" while pointing at the items.

The conversation should follow the example given on Sheet 4f. You could put prompts on the board in English suggesting what the pupils should say, for example, reminding them to start by greeting each other.

Introducing the phrase, "C'est combien, s'il vous plaît?" enables the children to practise numbers up to 10.

Vocabulaire

C'est combien, How much is
  s'il vous plaît? this, please?
en français in French
un euro a euro

Materials
★ Sheets 2c(i)–2c(ii) (pages 31–32) photocopied back-to-back and cut into cards, one set per pupil
★ Sheet 4f (page 56)
★ CD, Track 13

Note
The pupils will not yet have been introduced to plurals. If asked, explain that the plural of "euro" is pronounced the same as the singular even though is it written with an "s": "euros".

Materials

★ Sheet 4g (page 57)

Essential words and phrases

At the end of this unit, give the pupils Sheet 4g which will help them to remember essential words and phrases.

Au revoir!

Goodbye!

Remember always to wish the pupils a good week or weekend, depending on when the lesson takes place. Wait for them to reply, "Merci, Madame/Monsieur, vous aussi!" If the next lesson is on Tuesday (for example), you could say "À mardi!"

Nom:_____   **La date:**_____

A. Regarde et relie

Look and join each number with the correct word.

1	quatre
3	neuf
7	un
2	deux
10	zéro
4	huit
0	trois
6	cinq
8	six
5	sept
9	dix

B. Écris

Write the following numbers in letters.

0 _____   6 _____

1 _____   7 _____

2 _____   8 _____

3 _____   9 _____

4 _____   10 _____

5 _____

Nom:_____   **La date:**_____

Cootie catcher

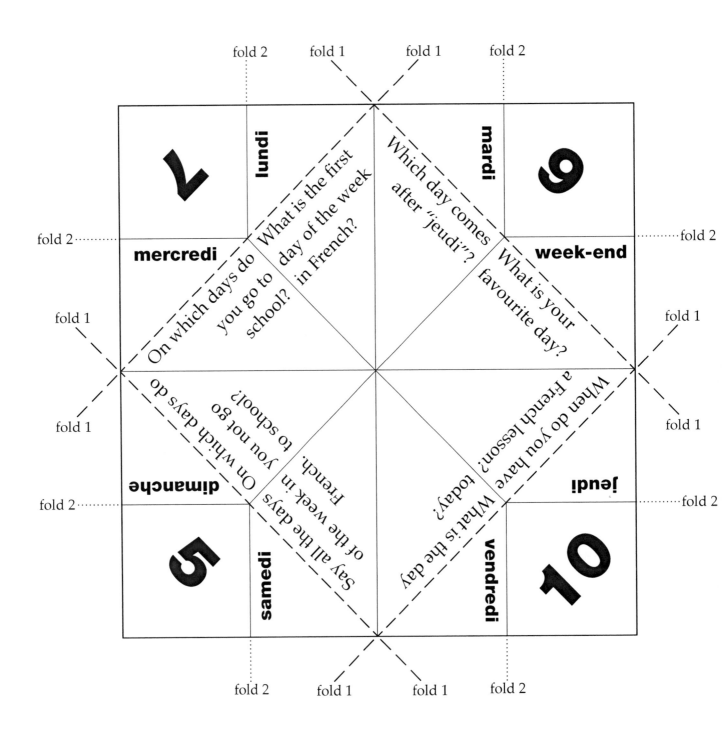

1. Fold corners **back** behind face of paper along fold 1: — — — —
2. Fold corners **inward** to centre along fold 2: ·················
3. Put your thumb and forefinger of both hands into the back of the resulting square and pinch up into a point.

Nom:_____ **La date:**_____

A. Trouve

Find the days of the week and the French word for "today" in this word search.

j	e	u	d	i	i	d	n	s	a
o	s	d	i	d	n	u	l	u	u
u	d	i	e	e	l	b	j	o	r
r	i	m	a	r	u	o	h	u	e
d	a	a	m	c	u	n	n	e	v
s	o	n	v	r	o	j	n	b	o
s	a	c	d	e	v	o	u	r	i
r	d	h	a	m	c	u	i	d	r
j	u	e	s	m	a	r	d	i	i
i	d	e	r	d	n	e	v	e	s

lundi
mardi
mercredi
jeudi
vendredi
samedi
dimanche
aujourd'hui

The French words for "hello" and "goodbye" are also in the word search. Can you find them?

B. Trouve et écris

Find and write the missing days on the following lists.

1.   lundi, mardi, _____, jeudi, vendredi, samedi, dimanche

2.   vendredi, _____, dimanche, lundi, _____, mercredi

3.   mardi, mercredi, _____, vendredi, _____, dimanche

C. Trouve et colorie

Find and colour the days of the week.

1.   M A R L U N D I D O U C I

2.   J U I L S A M E D I V E N L A T I O N

3.   I N F O M A J O U I J E U D I L E

4.   L U N A D I M A N C H E P U C I T

Nom:_____ **La date:**_____

Regarde et réponds

Look at the drawings and answer the questions using "c'est".

1. Qu'est-ce que c'est?

2. Qu'est-ce que c'est?

_____

3. Qu'est-ce que c'est?

4. Qu'est-ce que c'est?

_____

5. Qu'est-ce que c'est?

6. Qu'est-ce que c'est?

_____

7. Qu'est-ce que c'est?

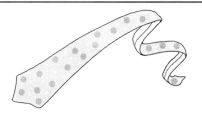

8. Qu'est-ce que c'est?

_____

9. Qu'est-ce que c'est?

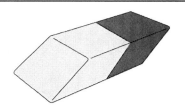

10. Qu'est-ce que c'est?

_____

Nom:_____ **La date:**_____

It is good to be the king!

Hexagonie was such a big kingdom that it needed an important king to rule the country. The king of Hexagonie was called "Le Roi Être" which meant "King To Be".

King Être lived with the queen in their beautiful palace. He was good at being king and was respected by all the nouns who were his subjects.

Depending on the occasion King Être knew how to be kind and happy as well as firm and strict if necessary. Even though he could also be grumpy at times, all the nouns could not "be" without him. It was thanks to him that they existed.

Every noun in the kingdom dreamed of being introduced to King Être. And when they had the good fortune of being granted an audience with the king, the nouns could not believe it! They would repeat over and over "C'est incroyable! Ce n'est pas possible!" ("It's incredible! It's not possible!")

During the meeting, the king would be seated on his magnificent golden throne, on which was engraved: "Le Roi, c'est moi!" ("The King, it's me!"). The king would always start the conversation asking, "Qui es-tu?" ("Who are you?") and the nouns would respectfully say their names, replying, "Je suis une lampe," "Je suis un coussin."

After their royal audience, the nouns would be so happy to have met King Être that for months afterwards they would talk about it proudly.

Nom:_____ **La date:**_____

Lis

Read this dialogue that takes place in a clothes shop.

Nom:_____ **La date:**_____

Essential words and phrases

How to ask what something is

Qu'est-ce que c'est?	What is it?
Qu'est-ce que c'est en français?	What is it in French?

How to ask how much something costs

C'est combien, s'il vous plaît?	How much is this, please?

The days of the week

lundi	Monday	from the French word "lune" (moon)
mardi	Tuesday	from "Mars" (Mars)
mercredi	Wednesday	from "Mercure" (Mercury)
jeudi	Thursday	from "Jupiter" (Jupiter)
vendredi	Friday	from "Vénus" (Venus)
samedi	Saturday	
dimanche	Sunday	

How to say "See you on Monday/Tuesday" etc.

À lundi!	See you on Monday!
À mardi!	See you on Tuesday!
À mercredi!	See you on Wednesday!
À jeudi!	See you on Thursday!
À vendredi!	See you on Friday!
À samedi!	See you on Saturday!
À dimanche!	See you on Sunday!

Note

The days of the week do not start with a capital letter in French.

Unit 5

Some nouns are different

Vocabulaire

Comment vas-tu?	How are you?
Je vais bien, merci	I am well, thank you
Je ne vais pas bien	I am not well
comme çi, comme ça	so-so
moi aussi	me too

Materials

★ "Je vais bien…" (page 199)
★ CD, Track 14

Bonjour, comment vas-tu?

Hello, how are you?

Say "Bonjour" to the whole class waiting for the pupils to reply "Bonjour, Madame/Monsieur".

Before calling the register, tell the whole class that when people who know each other meet they often ask each other, "Comment vas-tu?" which means, "How are you?" Tell them that you are going to practise this question with them and that they have to answer, "Je vais bien, merci," which means, "I am well, thank you." To help them memorize this social skill, hold up the sheet (page 199) on which the sentence is written.

Call the register (in the same way as in previous units). After every pupil responds "présent(e)" ask, "Comment vas-tu?" waiting for, "Je vais bien, merci." In subsequent units you can vary using "Comment vas-tu?" and "Ça va bien?" You should also introduce "Je ne vais pas bien," and "Comme çi, comme ça."

In Track 14, Monsieur Grand, Madame Petite and Mademoiselle Jolie greet each other. By now they have become friends and use "tu" when speaking to each other.

Ask for volunteers to perform a similar dialogue, imagining that two pupils meet and greet each other in the street, asking how the other is, for example:

Bonjour Zack!

Bonjour Gabriella!

Comment vas-tu aujourd'hui?

Je vais bien, merci, et toi?

Moi aussi, je vais bien.

Recap on "Qu'est-ce que c'est?"

Tell a pupil to take a flashcard from a small bag and ask, "Qu'est-ce que c'est?" to another pupil of his/her choice, who answers and then does the same.

Materials

★ Flashcards of whatever vocabulary you would like the pupils to practise
★ Small bag

Rhyming words

Hold up a pen and ask the pupils "Qu'est-ce que c'est?" They will answer "un stylo". Write "un stylo" on the board and point out the "o" at the end of the word. Tell the pupils that in French the sound "o" is sometimes spelled differently. Ask them if they can think of any other words they have learned ending in an "o" sound. They might think of:

un couteau	a knife
un manteau	a coat
un chapeau	a hat
un bureau	a desk

Vocabulaire

Va au tableau!	Go to the board!
un bateau	a boat
un oiseau	a bird
un gâteau	a cake
un cadeau	a present
un château	a castle

Materials

★ Sheet 5a (page 62)
★ CD, Track 15

This is a good opportunity to introduce the word for "(black) board" : "un tableau" (if you did not introduce it in Unit 4). Explain that "Va au tableau!" means, "Go to the (black) board!" You could give several pupils opportunities to go to the board, saying, "Va au tableau!" to practise this phrase.

5a

Ask the pupils to complete the rhyming quiz on Sheet 5a either in the class or at home. It introduces some new words, but will help them to understand the connection between spelling and pronounciation.

Track 15

Sheet 5a can also be done as a listening activity using Track 15 on the CD.

Materials

★ Sheet 5b (page 63)

Hexagonie story

Give each pupil a copy of Sheet 5b: "The bad old days", and ask a pupil to read it out loud. Wait for their comments and discuss to reinforce the points covered.

Ask the pupils what "memory tricks" the story gives them for remembering nouns that are exceptions to the male/female rule. The children could draw pictures to illustrate the memory tricks to help them remember the exceptions.

Vocabulaire

une télévision	a television
une maison	a house
une fleur	a flower
un livre	a book
un dictionnaire	a dictionary
une question	a question

Materials

★ Sheet 5c (page 64)

Les exceptions

Nouns that are exceptions

Draw two columns on the blackboard, one entitled "un" and the other "une". Call out a word from the *Vocabulaire* list without "un" or "une" and ask the pupils individually to tell you if it takes "un" or "une". All these words are exceptions to the rule that words ending in "e" are usually feminine.

Explain that the memory trick for remembering that "télévision" is feminine is incredibly useful as you can use it to remember whether lots of other words are feminine or not. In French, almost all words ending in "-ion", like "télévision", are feminine, such as "question". Two other words like this that are introduced in Unit 14 are "natation" ("swimming") and "équitation" ("horse riding").

Ask the pupils to match each noun with "un" or "une" on Sheet 5c. This sheet has some nouns that are exceptions to the rule and some that are not.

Je voudrais...

I would like…

Tell the pupils that they are now going to act out going to "une boulangerie" – a bakery. They will need to use the phrases "Je voudrais..." ("I would like...") and "Voilà" ("Here it is"), as well as "S'il vous plaît" and "C'est combien?" which were introduced in Units 3 and 4.

The children will probably already be familiar with the words "baguette" and "croissant". You could also introduce "un pain" and "un pain au chocolat".

Divide the pupils into pairs. Give each group a copy of Sheet 5d, and ask each group to prepare a role-play to perform in front of the class. Encourage them to make their characters different in some way. They should practise the role-play swapping characters. After they are performed, decide which role-play was the best and give every pupil in the winning group a "Tableau d'Honneur".

Ask the pupils to do Sheet 5e in the class or at home.

Track 16 provides three mini-dialogue listening exercises that take place in a shop.

Vocabulaire

une boulangerie	a bakery
je voudrais…	I would like…
voilà	here it is
une baguette	a baguette
un croissant	a croissant
un pain	a loaf of bread
un pain au chocolat	a pastry with chocolate filling

Materials

★ Flashcards of une baguette, un croissant, un pain and un pain au chocolat
★ Sheet 5d (page 65), one copy per pair
★ Tableau d'Honneur (page 203)
★ Sheet 5e (page 66)
★ CD, Track 16

Essential words and phrases

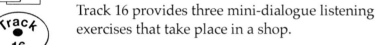

At the end of this unit, give the pupils Sheet 5f, which will help them to remember essential words and phrases.

Materials

★ Sheet 5f (page 67)

Au revoir!

Remember always to wish the pupils a good week or weekend, depending on when the lesson takes place. Wait for them to reply "Merci, Madame/Monsieur, vous aussi!" If the next lesson is on Thursday (for example), you could say "À jeudi!"

Nom:_____   **La date:**_____

Regarde 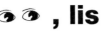 , lis et réponds

All the words on this sheet end with the sound "o". See if you can answer the questions using the picture clues and the words you already know.

1. Qu'est-ce que c'est?

    C'est un bat**eau** ou un styl**o**?

    _____

2. Qu'est-ce que c'est?

    C'est un cout**eau** ou un ois**eau**?

    _____

3. Qu'est-ce que c'est?

    C'est un bat**eau** ou un gât**eau**?

    _____

4. Qu'est-ce que c'est?

    C'est un chât**eau** ou un chap**eau**?

    _____

5. Qu'est-ce que c'est?

    C'est un cad**eau** ou un mant**eau**?

    _____

6. Qu'est-ce que c'est?

    C'est un chât**eau** ou un ois**eau**?

    _____

Nom:＿＿＿＿＿＿＿＿＿＿＿＿＿＿＿＿＿＿＿＿＿＿ **La date:**＿＿＿＿＿＿＿＿＿＿＿＿＿＿＿

The bad old days

Hexagonie has not always been a perfect kingdom. In fact, a long, long time ago, in "the bad old days", the girl nouns were not allowed to go to school and had to stay at home all day. That is why the noun for house, "maison", became a female noun.

However, the boy nouns – lucky boys! – were allowed to go to school and learn about lots of new nouns in a big book called "dictionnaire" (dictionary). How wonderful for them! That is why the noun for book, "livre", was made a male noun as well.

However, the girls nouns were determined not to remain in the house doing nothing. No way! First they watched television all day but their mothers could not stand seeing them inactive so they encouraged them to go outside and to discover the wonderful world of nature. So the girl nouns started to have fun outside and grew all sorts of beautiful flowers in their gardens. The kingdom became very pretty and the girl nouns were very proud of their flowers. That is why the noun for flower, "fleur", became a female noun.

Then something even more amazing happened! Because the girl nouns used to watch television all the time, the noun "télévision" became female. But not only that, most other nouns ending in "ion", such as "question" became female as well. What a great achievement for the girl nouns!

Nom:_____   **La date:**_____

Lis et relie

Read and join

Match up the words with either "un" or "une".

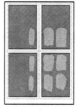

fenêtre

maison

armoire

fauteuil

un

fleur

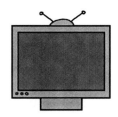

télévision

une

livre

ordinateur

dictionnaire

lit

Nom:_____ **La date:**_____

Lis

Read

The customer (you start the conversation)

• Greet the salesperson.

• Ask the salesperson for a type of bread of your choice using "Je voudrais…"

• Ask the salesperson, "C'est combien?"

• Pay the salesperson, saying "Voilà!"

• Thank the salesperson, say goodbye and wish him/her a good day.

The salesperson

• Greet the customer.

• When giving the customer what he/she wants, say "Voilà!"

• Tell the customer how must it costs in euros. Use numbers 1–10.

• Thank the customer and say goodbye.

This page may be photocopied for use by the purchasing institution only. © Maria Rice-Jones and Brilliant Publications

Nom:_____ **La date:**_____

Regarde et relie

Look and join the children to the things they would like.

1.

Je voudrais une fleur.

2.

Je voudrais un pyjama.

3.

Je voudrais une plante.

4.

Je voudrais un ordinateur.

5.

Je voudrais un cadeau.

6.

Je voudrais une télévision.

7.

Je voudrais un gâteau.

8.

Je voudrais un livre.

Nom:_____   **La date:**_____

Essential words and phrases

How to ask how somebody is

Comment vas-tu?   How are you?

How to reply

Je vais bien.   I am well.

Je ne vais pas bien.   I am not well.

Comme çi, comme ça.   So-so.

Useful shopping phrases

Je voudrais…   I would like…

C'est combien, s'il vous   How much is it, please?
   plaît?

Voilà!   Here it is!

How the teacher asks a pupil to go to the board

Va au tableau!   Go to the board!

Unit 6

Be precise with "the"

Key teaching points/vocabulary

The definite article ("the")
Rooms in the house
"De quelle couleur est…?" ("What colour is…?')
Fruit

Bonjour

Say "Bonjour" to the whole class, waiting for the pupils to reply, "Bonjour, Madame/Monsieur."

Call the register, and ask at random, "Comment vas-tu?" or "Ça va bien?" waiting for the pupil to reply, "Je vais bien, merci," or "Ça va bien, merci."

Recap on "je voudrais…" and "voilà!"

Vocabulaire	
s'il te plaît	please (to a friend/child)

Tell a pupil to ask another pupil of his/her choice for something. For example, "Bonjour Rebecca, je voudrais un livre bleu, s'il te plaît." (If necessary explain that "s'il te plaît" is how you say "please" to a friend or child.) Rebecca pretends she is giving the object requested and replies, "Voilà un livre bleu." Then Rebecca asks another pupil the same type of question with another item, and so on.

Hexagonie story

Materials

★ Sheet 6a (page 73)

6a

Give the pupils Sheet 6a: "The precise noun", the next instalment in the Hexagonie story. Discuss to reinforce the points covered.

"Le" and "la"

Vocabulaire

le soleil	the sun
la lune	the moon

The

Draw a sun and a moon on the board and point to them and say, "C'est le soleil, c'est la lune".

Write "c'est le soleil" under the sun and "c'est la lune" under the moon, asking the pupils to tell you what each word means. They will certainly say, "It's the sun," and "It's the moon," realizing that "le" and "la" both mean "the".

Underneath "le soleil" write other masculine words, for example "le miroir", "le lit", and underneath "la lune" write other feminine words, for example "la table", "la cuillère".

"L' "

The

Vocabulaire

une étoile	a star
un homme	a man
une école	a school
une église	a church

Draw a star on the board and write "l'étoile" (the star) under it. Underline the first letter "é". Tell the pupils that when a word starts with a vowel it is preceded by "l' " because the French find it easier to pronounce.

Underneath the word "l'étoile" write other words they have already been introduced to, starting with a vowel, such as:

l'assiette

l'armoire

l'oiseau

l'ordinateur

Introduce "l'homme" (the man) and "l'horloge" (a clock) to show how this rule applies to some common words starting with "h" as well.

Recap by writing:

le	+	soleil	
la	+	lune	
l'	+	étoile	

Note

You may substitute the words for others of your choice, for example: "école", "église" or "ami", but avoid exceptions to the masculine/feminine rule to avoid confusion.

Vocabulaire

un salon	a sitting room
une cuisine	a kitchen
une salle à manger	a dining room
une entrée	an entrance hall
une cave	a cellar
un grenier	a loft (attic)
une chambre	a bedroom
une salle de bains	a bathroom
dans	in

Materials

★ Flashcards of rooms in the house and items of furniture – you could make them from Sheets 6b(i)–6b(ii) (pages 74–75)
★ Sheets 6b(i)–6b(ii) (pages 74–75), one copy of each per group
★ Pair of scissors and three envelopes per group
★ Tableau d'Honneur (page 203)
★ Sheet 6c (page 76)
★ CD, Track 17

Les pièces de la maison

Rooms in the house

Remind the pupils of the Hexagonie story for this unit. In it "la porte" wanted everyone to know that she was "la porte dans la cuisine" – the door in the kitchen.

Use flashcards to introduce the words for rooms in the house. You could ask individual children to point to things in the rooms and say, for example, "C'est le lit dans la chambre." Flashcards showing pictures of household items might be useful here.

Divide the pupils into groups of four and give each group three envelopes. On the first envelope ask the pupils to write "le", on the second envelope "la", and on the third "l' ". Give each group a copy of Sheets 6b(i) and 6b(ii). Ask them to write "le", "la" and "l' " onto the sheets then cut up the cards and put each one in the appropriate envelope. If a group succeeds in getting them all right, reward them with a "Tableau d'Honneur".

Ask the pupils to complete Sheet 6c in the class or at home.

You will need the following flashcards for this activity:

Number	Room
61	le salon
62	la cuisine
63	la salle à manger
64	l'entrée
65	la cave
66	le grenier
67	la chambre
68	la salle de bains

Note:
The numbers relate to the set of flashcards that can be bought separately.

Hold up the cards in order, as instructed on the CD, so that all the children can see them. Encourage them to respond in full sentences in the pauses.

C'est un citron

It's a lemon

Hand out pieces of fruit to some of the pupils. Ask each pupil to point at their item in turn and ask you, "Qu'est-ce que c'est, Madame/Monsieur?"

Tell them what it is, for example, "C'est un citron." You could add the colour if you think it is appropriate by saying, "C'est un citron jaune."

Ask the children to pass their piece of fruit to a different person after asking you the question, so that everyone has several goes.

Once you feel that the pupils are familiar with the new vocabulary, gather up the pieces of fruit, then hold them up at random and ask "Qu'est-ce que c'est?" waiting for all the pupils to answer in chorus.

6d

Ask the pupils to draw what is indicated on Sheet 6d.

Vocabulaire

un citron	a lemon
une pomme	an apple
une poire	a pear
une orange	an orange
un ananas	a pineapple
une banane	a banana
une cerise	a cherry
un kiwi	a kiwi

Materials

★ Pieces of fruit
★ Sheet 6d (page 77)

De quelle couleur est...?

What colour is...?"

Point at something in the classroom, such as a table, a chair or a door, and ask the pupils its colour by saying, "De quelle couleur est la table?" Wait for the pupils to answer in chorus, "La table est brune." Then do the same with more items.

Using flashcards of your choice, hold up one, the lemon for example, and ask the class, "De quelle couleur est le citron?" waiting for the pupils to answer, "Le citron est jaune." Then do the same with the other cards.

Encourage the pupils to ask you the colour of different objects. They should use, "De quelle couleur est...?" to ask the question.

Always remember to congratulate a correct answer with an enthusiastic "Très bien!", "Excellent!" or "Bravo!"

Perform a Mexican wave where every pupil asks the colour of an item, for example:

Rachel: Alina, de quelle couleur est la chaise?
Alina: La chaise est verte. Tom, de quelle couleur est le crayon?
Tom: Le crayon est rouge.

And so on.

Vocabulaire

De quelle couleur est...?	What colour is...?

Materials

★ Flashcards of whatever vocabulary you wish to practise
★ Sheet 6e (page 78)
★ CD, Track 16
★ Coloured pencils

Ask the pupils to answer the questions and to colour the pictures on Sheet 6e. They will need to decide on a colour for each item. Encourage them to use as many colours as possible.

In Track 18, Le Roi Être quizzes the other characters about the colours of his favourite fruits.

Materials

★ Sheet 6f (page 79)

Essential words and phrases

At the end of this unit, give the pupils Sheet 6f, which will help them to remember essential words and phrases.

Au revoir!

Remember always to wish the pupils a good week or weekend depending on when the lesson takes place. Wait for them to reply, "Merci, Madame/Monsieur, vous aussi!" If the next lesson is on Friday (for example), you could say, "À vendredi!" and encourage the pupils to answer back, "À vendredi!"

Nom:_____   **La date:**_____

The precise noun

In Hexagonie, there were many regions and towns, and all the nouns came from different areas of the kingdom. For example, "porte" lived in the house area, while "cahier" came from the classroom area, and "fleur" lived in the garden area.

Whenever the nouns introduced themselves to other nouns, they always wanted to be precise about who they were. So a door would want others to know exactly which door she was and not take her for just any old door. Therefore, she would say, "Hello, I am the door from the kitchen, in the house area." By using the word "the" she was able to be more precise about her identity.

The nouns couldn't agree on the best way to say "the", so there were three different ways of saying "the" before one noun: "le", "la" and "l' ".

When a female noun referred to herself, she used "la": "la jupe" or "la porte". She chose the letter "a" because she thought it must be the most important letter of the alphabet, as it comes first.

The male noun wanted to be different from the female noun so he chose to refer to himself using "le", such as "le short" or "le pull-over".

But when a noun started with a vowel or an "h" the female and male nouns all agreed that it sounded much better to start with "l' " such as "l'oiseau" (the bird) or "l'armoire".

So at least the male and female nouns were able to agree on something!

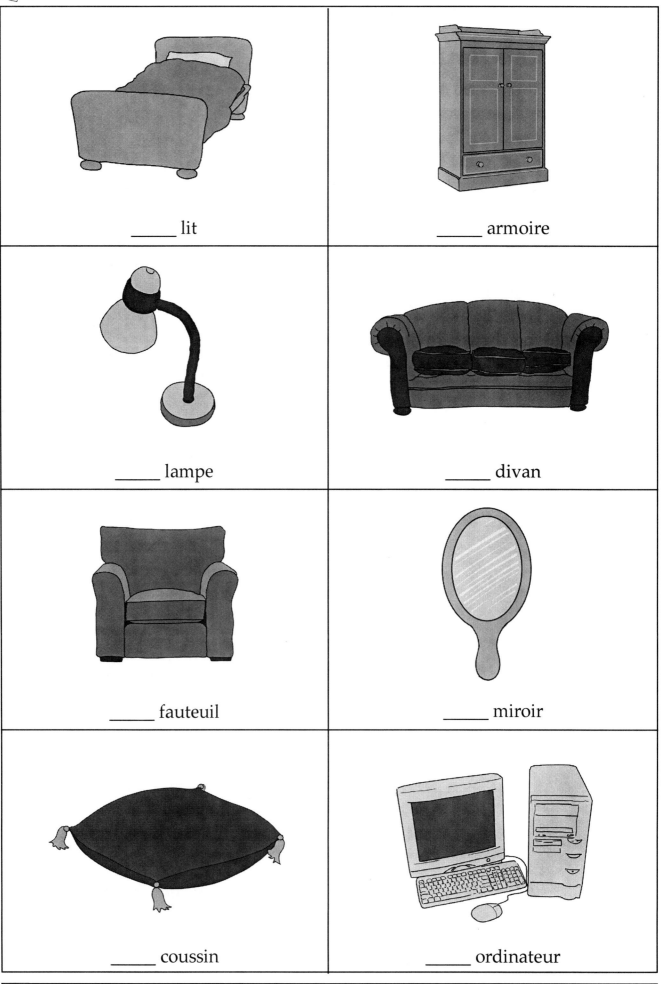

_____ lit

_____ armoire

_____ lampe

_____ divan

_____ fauteuil

_____ miroir

_____ coussin

_____ ordinateur

_____ salon

_____ cuisine

_____ salle à manger

_____ salle de bains

_____ chambre

_____ entréé

_____ cave

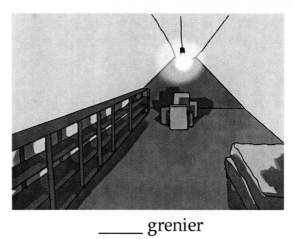

_____ grenier

Nom:_____   **La date:**_____

Complète

Fill in the gaps with "le", "la", or "l' ".

1. C'est _____ étoile.

2. C'est _____ chemise.

3. C'est _____ château.

4. C'est _____ croissant.

4. C'est _____ chambre de Sophie.

5. C'est _____ horloge.

7. C'est _____ pyjama.

8. C'est _____ maison.

Nom:_____   **La date:**_____

Lis 📖 et dessine 🎨

Read and draw

1. C'est la pomme.	2. C'est le citron.
3. C'est l'orange.	4. C'est la poire.
5. C'est l'ananas.	6. C'est la banane.
7. C'est le kiwi.	8. C'est la cerise.

Nom:_____   **La date:**_____

Colorie et réponds

Colour the pictures with at least five different colours, then answer the questions.

1. De quelle couleur est le manteau?

    _____

2. De quelle couleur est l'orange?

    _____

3. De quelle couleur est la règle?

    _____

4. De quelle couleur est le pantalon?

    _____

5. De quelle couleur est la cerise?

    _____

6. De quelle couleur est le divan?

    _____

7. De quelle couleur est la banane?

    _____

8. De quelle couleur est l'oiseau?

    _____

9. De quelle couleur est le dictionnaire?

    _____

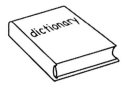

Nom:_____   **La date:**_____

Essential words and phrases

How to say "the"

le (+ masculine noun, starting with a consonant), e.g. "le soleil"

la (+ feminine noun, starting with a consonant), e.g. "la lune"

l' (+ any noun, masculine or feminine, starting with a vowel), e.g. "l'étoile"

How to ask the colour of something

De quelle couleur est…?   What colour is…?

How to say "please"

s'il te plaît   please (to a friend/child)

s'il vous plaît   please (to the teacher)

Unit 7

"Est-ce que...?" is asking you a question!

Key teaching points/vocabulary

Question words
"Être" ("to be") with "je", "tu" and "il/elle"
Negative sentences
Sentences with "parce que" ("because")
Prepositions

Bonjour

Say "Bonjour" to the whole class, waiting for the pupils to reply, "Bonjour, Madame/Monsieur." Call the register, and ask at random, "Comment vas-tu?" or "Ça va bien?"

Vocabulaire

Qu'est-ce qui est...?	What is...?
la salle	the room

Recap on "le", "la" and "l' "

Ask the pupils to tell you what in the classroom is blue by saying, "Qu'est-ce qui est bleu dans la salle?" Repeat with other colours. The pupils should give answers such as, "La fenêtre est bleue," or "Le cahier est vert." Make sure they use "le", "la" and "l' " correctly.

Congratulate a correct answer with an enthusiastic, "C'est très bien!"

Vocabulaire

Est-ce que...?	*introduces a question*
n'est pas	isn't

Materials

★ Sheet 7a (page 87)

"Est-ce que" introduces a question

 Write "Est-ce que...?" and "question" on the board and underline the many letters they have in common.

Tell the pupils that "Est-ce que...?" introduces a question. Get them used to the sound of "Est-ce que...?" by repeating it several times, with the pupils saying it after you in chorus. You can make this more entertaining by asking them to use different types of voices, e.g. loud, soft, funny, angry.

Ask, "Est-ce que le plafond est blanc?" (point to the ceiling as a hint) and wait for the pupils to answer in chorus, "Oui, le plafond est blanc."

Tell the pupils that "Est-ce que...?" is like an alarm bell to make them wake up and listen carefully to the question! Tell them not to try to translate "Est-ce que...?" because the literal translation would be "Is it that...?" which does not help at all.

Point at different things in the room, asking the whole class questions beginning with "Est-ce que...?" Introduce some questions where "Est-ce que" precedes a word starting with a vowel, for example: "Est-ce qu'il est grand ou petit?" After a while you can introduce some questions that will require a negative answer, e.g. "Est-ce que le plafond est noir?" Prompt the children to reply, "Non, le plafond n'est pas noir."

Perform a Mexican wave with questions such as:

Daniel:	Chen, est-ce que le crayon est bleu?
Chen:	Oui, le crayon est bleu.
	Maddie, est-ce que la porte est verte?
Maddie:	Non, la porte n'est pas verte.
	Louise, est-ce que la table est brune?
Louise:	Oui, la table est brune.

7a Ask the pupils to complete the activity on Sheet 7a either in the class or at home.

Hexagonie story

7b Give the pupils Sheet 7b: "The Est-ce Que Officers", the next instalment in the Hexagonie story. Discuss to reinforce the points covered.

Materials

★ Sheet 7b (page 88)

Je suis, tu es, il/elle est

I am, you are, he/she is

Say, "Je ne suis pas petit(e) parce que je suis grand(e)," while miming "grand(e)" and "petit(e)". Repeat this sentence two or three times and ask the pupils to tell you what it means.

 Write on the board:
I am
you are
he is
she is

Explain that just as you say "I am" instead of "I is" in English, so there are different words for "am" and "is" in French too. Write them on the board as well:

I am	je suis
you are	tu es
he is	il est
she is	elle est

Vocabulaire

grand(e)	big/tall
petit(e)	small/short
parce que	because
je suis	I am
tu es	you are
il est	he is
elle est	she is

Vocabulaire

stupide	stupid
intelligent(e)	intelligent
gentil(le)	nice/friendly
méchant(e)	naughty
riche	rich
pauvre	poor
joli(e)	pretty
laid(e)	ugly
pourquoi?	why?

Materials

★ Sheet 7c (page 89) cut into cards, one set per pupil
★ CD, Track 19

Negative form "ne… pas"

Explain that in French, unlike in English, we use two words to say "not". These words are "ne" and "pas". "Ne" always goes before the verb and "pas" after the verb. If necessary point out where the verb is.

On the board, write "ne" and "pas" in red for "je", "tu", "il" and "elle". Explain that "ne" changes into "n' " when it precedes a verb starting with a vowel:

je suis	je **ne** suis **pas**
tu es	tu **n'**es **pas**
il est	il **n'**est **pas**
elle est	elle **n'**est **pas**

Tell the pupils to imagine that "ne" and "pas" are two prison walls, which lock up one verb only.

Say sentences such as "Je ne suis pas stupide parce que je suis intelligent(e)," or "Je ne suis pas petit(e) parce que je suis grand(e)." After each sentence ask the pupils to tell you what it means.

Encourage pupils to make up simple positive and negative sentences of their own, e.g. "Je suis grand(e)," or "Je ne suis pas petit(e)." Ask them "Pourquoi?" and prompt them to answer using "parce que…".

7c

Give each pupil a set of prompt cards made from Sheet 7c showing opposites, and ask the pupils to make up phrases about themselves using opposite adjectives, for example, "Je ne suis pas grand(e) parce que je suis petit(e)." If you feel your pupils are ready, you could ask them to make up similar phrases about others using "tu", "il" and "elle".

Tell the pupils to listen carefully to Track 19 on the CD and answer the questions in the pauses.

Note
Some children might now realize that the characters on the CD have very descriptive names: Monsieur Grand is Mr Tall, Madame Petite is Mrs Small and Mademoiselle Jolie is Miss Pretty.

La France

France

Give the pupils Sheet 7d. Read the sentences in French at the top together and discuss them.

Ask the children to use an atlas or a map to label the bordering countries on their sheet (in French).

To memorize which countries share a border with France, put the first letter of each country together to make the words "is" and "able" and remember "France is able!"

L'**I**talie
La **S**uisse
L'**A**llemagne
La **B**elgique
Le **L**uxembourg
L'**E**spagne

Vocabulaire

un pays	a country
une capitale	a capital
L'Italie	Italy
La Suisse	Switzerland
L'Allemagne	Germany
La Belgique	Belgium
Le Luxembourg	Luxembourg
L'Espagne	Spain

Materials

★ Sheet 7d (page 90)
★ Atlas or map

Les prépositions

Prepositions

Stand behind your desk, holding a pen, and ask the following question to the class, miming the two options so that the pupils understand that "devant" means "in front" and "derrière" means "behind": "Est-ce que le stylo est devant moi ou derrière moi?"

Repeat this question two or three times and wait for the answer, "Le stylo est devant vous." (You may need to prompt them to use "vous".)

Stand in front of your desk with the wall behind you and ask, "Est-ce que le mur est devant moi ou derrière moi?" waiting for the answer, "Le mur est derrière vous."

Pretend to be looking for something, and introduce questions with "où", such as:

Teacher: Où est la gomme? Sur la chaise ou sur la table?
Pupils: La gomme est sur la table, devant vous.

Teacher: Où est le cahier? Sur la chaise ou sur la table?
Pupils: Le cahier est devant vous, sur la chaise.

Teacher: Où est le livre? Dans le sac ou sur la table?
Pupils: Le livre est dans le sac.

Ask the pupils to complete the activity on Sheet 7e, either in the class or at home.

Vocabulaire

devant	in front of
derrière	behind
sur	on top of
sous	under
dans	in
où	where
ou	or
Maman	Mummy
Papa	Daddy
un jardin	a garden
un bureau	an office / a desk

Materials

★ Sheets 7e and 7f (pages 91–92)

Ask the pupils to complete this activity. Explain that "Maman" means "Mummy" and "Papa" means "Daddy". The word "bureau" is used for both "office" (as on this sheet) and "desk" (as in Unit 3).

Vocabulaire

la classe	the classroom
en face de	opposite
à côté de	next to
moi	me
toi	you
lui	him
elle	her
Qui est…?	Who is…?
Qui suis-je?	Who am I?

Materials

★ Sheet 7g (page 93)
★ CD, Track 20

À coté de et en face de

Next to and opposite

Draw the following classroom "la classe" on the board:

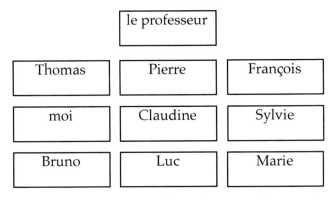

	le professeur	
Thomas	Pierre	François
moi	Claudine	Sylvie
Bruno	Luc	Marie

Ask the whole class questions about where these people are using "Où est…?" and wait for the answer. For example:

Teacher: Où est François?
Pupils: François est devant Sylvie.

Teacher: Où est Luc?
Pupils: Luc est derrière Claudine.

Teacher: Où est Sylvie?
Pupils: Sylvie est derrière François et devant Marie.

Teacher: Où est Claudine?
Pupils: Claudine est derrière Pierre et devant Luc.

Show the box with "moi" and say: "Je suis à côté de Claudine. Luc est à côté de Marie et de Bruno," etc.

Ask the class more questions about where people are, for example:

Teacher: Où est Marie?
Pupils: Marie est à côté de Luc.

Teacher: Où est Thomas?
Pupils: Thomas est à côté de Pierre.

Say, "Le professeur est en face de Pierre. Et maintenant, je suis en face de vous."

Ask questions about the different pupils using "Qui est...?" for example:

> Qui est à côté de Bruno? Luc ou Claudine?
> Qui est en face de Pierre?
> Qui est à côté de moi?

Say and write the following on the board:

derrière (behind)	moi
devant (in front of)	moi
à côté de (next to)	moi
en face de (opposite)	moi

Note
You could also introduce "toi" (you), "lui" (him) and "elle" (her).

Ask the pupils if they know why we say "derrière moi" and "devant moi", without "de", while with the other expressions we have to say the word "de", for example, "à côté de moi", "en face de moi".

Wait for their suggestions and tell them how it would be easy to remember:

There is no need to say "de" after "**de**vant" and "**de**rrière" because "de" is already part of the word.

Ask the pupils to use prepositions for the activity on Sheet 7g. Introduce the pupils to the phrase, "Qui suis-je?" prior to asking them to fill it in.

Sheet 7g can also be done as an oral activity using Track 20 on the CD.

Essential words and phrases

At the end of this unit, give the pupils Sheet 7h, which will help them to remember essential words and phrases.

Materials
★ Sheet 7h (page 94)

Vocabulaire

À bientôt!   See you soon!

Au revoir!

Remember always to wish the pupils a good week or weekend depending on when the lesson takes place. Wait for them to reply "Merci, Madame/Monsieur, vous aussi." Tell the children "À bientôt!" ("See you soon!") and encourage them to answer back with "À bientôt!"

Nom:_____ **La date:**_____

Lis et réponds

Read the questions and answer in full sentences, as done in the example.

e.g. Est-ce que c'est un citron?
Non, ce n'est pas un citron mais c'est une pomme.
Est-ce que c'est une pomme?
Oui, c'est une pomme.

1.   Est-ce que c'est une veste?

_____

2.   Est-ce que c'est un tableau?

_____

3.   Est-ce que c'est une bouteille?

_____

4.   Est-ce que c'est un pyjama?

_____

5.   Est-ce que c'est une fourchette?

_____

6.   Est-ce que c'est la lune?

_____

7.   Est-ce que c'est un kiwi?

_____

8.   Est-ce que c'est une ceinture?

_____

Nom:_____ **La date:**_____

The "Est-ce Que" Officers

The inhabitants of Hexagonie were so numerous and diverse that they had to be controlled by police officers. The police officers made sure that the roads were safe and that no inhabitants were behaving too badly. When the police stopped a noun, they would ask many questions with "Est-ce que…" to find out more about the noun and to decide if he or she was misbehaving or not.

The kingdom would have been very disorganized without the police force. At least with all their endless questions, the officers knew most things about the inhabitants who did not behave properly, and this was reassuring for the others.

These police officers were called the "Est-ce Que" Officers and were easily recognizable because of their uniform on which the letters "ESK" were printed in bright letters. These letters stood for "Est-ce que" – it was too long to print the whole thing.

The "Est-ce Que" Officers patrolled around the town and were always ready to help, so that almost every noun in Hexagonie felt safer and happier because they were around.

grand(e)	**petit(e)**
stupid(e)	**intelligent(e)**
méchant(e)	**gentil(le)**
riche	**pauvre**
joli(e)	**laid(e)**

Nom:_____ **La date:**_____

Réponds et complète

La France est un grand pays d'Europe.
La capitale de la France est Paris.

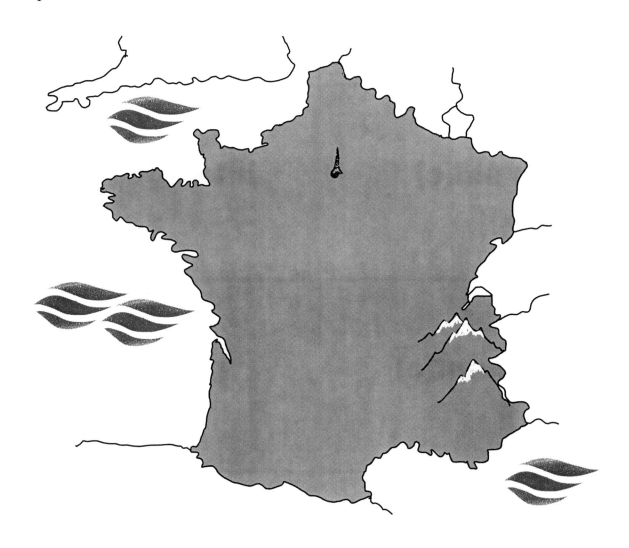

France shares borders with six other countries:

French names	English names
L'Italie	_____
La Suisse	_____
L'Allemagne	_____
La Belgique	_____
Le Luxembourg	_____
L'Espagne	_____

Use an atlas or a map to find out what these countries
are called in English and label them on the map
in French.

In which of these countries do people speak French?

Nom:_____ **La date:**_____

Regarde et réponds

Look at the pictures and answer the questions in full sentences.

1. Est-ce que le citron est sur le bureau ou sur le lit?

    _____

2. Est-ce que le gâteau est sur la table ou sous la table?

    _____

3. Est-ce que le kiwi est dans le livre ou sous le livre?

    _____

4. Est-ce que la cuillère est sur l'assiette ou sous
    l'assiette?

    _____

5. Est-ce que la poire est sur la chaise ou sous la chaise?

    _____

6. Est-ce que le crayon est sur le dictionnaire ou dans le
    dictionnaire?

    _____

Nom:_____ **La date:**_____

Réponds

Answer the questions.

grenier	salle de bains
chambre	bureau
salon	cuisine
salle à manger	
cave	jardin

e.g. Où est Maman? *Maman est dans la cuisine.*

1. Où est Papa? _____

2. Où est la télévision? _____

3. Où est la lampe? _____

4. Où est le tableau? _____

5. Où est l'ordinateur? _____

6. Où est Marie? _____

7. Où est Matthieu? _____

8. Où est la table? _____

Nom:_____   **La date:**_____

Regarde et réponds

Look at the layout of this classroom and answer the questions.

le professeur

Jean-Pierre	Luc	Christophe

Julie	Hélène	Aurélie

Daniel	Henri	Anne

e.g. Julie est devant moi. Qui suis-je?

Je suis Daniel.

1   Henri est derrière moi. Qui suis-je?

_____

2.   Anne est à côté de moi. Qui suis-je?

_____

3.   Henri est à côté de moi et Aurélie est devant moi. Qui suis-je?

_____

4.   Le professeur est en face de moi. Qui suis-je?

_____

5.   Christophe est devant moi et Anne est derrière moi. Qui suis-je?

_____

6.   Luc est à côté de moi et Julie est derrière moi. Qui suis-je?

_____

7.   Hélène est à côté de moi et Jean-Pierre est devant moi. Qui suis-je?

_____

8.   Luc est à côté de moi et Aurélie est derrière moi. Qui suis-je?

_____

Nom:_____ **La date:**_____

Essential words and phrases

How to ask "What is...?"

Qu'est-ce qui est...?   What is...?

How to introduce a question

Est-ce que...?   *introduces a question*

How to ask "why"

Pourquoi?   Why?

How to say "because"

parce que   because

How to talk about the position of things

devant moi   in front of me
devant toi   in front of you
derrière lui   behind him
derrière elle   behind her
en face de moi   opposite me
en face de toi   opposite you
à côté de lui   next to him
à côté d'elle   next to her

How to say "see you soon!"

À bientôt!   See you soon!

"Vive la différence!": nationalities

Key teaching points/vocabulary

Nationalities

"De quelle nationalité est...?" ("What is the nationality of...?")

Bonjour

Say "Bonjour" to the whole class waiting for the pupils to reply, "Bonjour, Madame/Monsieur." Call the register, and ask at random, "Comment vas-tu?" or "Ça va bien?"

Recap on "Est-ce que..."

Tell a pupil to ask another pupil of his/her choice any question using "Est-ce que..." and "tu es/il est/elle est". For example, "Est-ce que tu es devant moi?", "Est-ce que John est grand?" etc. The other pupil has to answer, and then ask the same type of question to another pupil of his/her choice and so on.

Les nationalités

Nationalities

Say: "Je suis Madame/Monsieur (your name). Je ne suis pas français(e) mais je suis anglais(e) (or whatever your nationality is)."

Use flashcards 77–81 (pages 224–226) showing couples from different countries and ask the pupils questions about each card as follows:

Flashcard 77 – English

Teacher:	Est-ce que Phillip est italien ou anglais?
Pupils:	Phillip est anglais.
Teacher:	Est-ce que Hannah est italienne ou anglaise?
Pupils:	Hannah est anglaise.

Flashcard 78 – French

Teacher:	Est-ce que Jacques est français ou pakistanais?
Pupils:	Jacques est français.
Teacher:	Est-ce que Céline est française ou pakistanaise?
Pupils:	Céline est française.

Flashcard 79 – American

Teacher:	Est-ce que Robert est américain ou chinois?
Pupils:	Robert est américain.

Vocabulaire

allemand(e)	German
américain(e)	American
anglais(e)	English
belge	Belgian
brésilien(ne)	Brazilian
canadien(ne)	Canadian
chinois(e)	Chinese
écossais(e)	Scottish
espagnol(e)	Spanish
français(e)	French
gallois(e)	Welsh
indien(ne)	Indian
irlandais(e)	Irish
italien(ne)	Italian
japonais(e)	Japanese
marocain(e)	Moroccan
pakistanais(e)	Pakistani
polonais(e)	Polish
portugais(e)	Portuguese

Materials

★ Flashcards 77–81 (pages 224–226)

Teacher: Est-ce que Sarah est américaine ou chinoise?
Pupils: Sarah est américaine.

Flashcard 80 – Japanese

Teacher: Est-ce que Hirotsugu est polonais ou japonais?
Pupils: Hirotsugu est japonais.

Teacher: Est-ce que Kanaï est polonaise or japonaise?
Pupils: Kanaï est japonaise.

Flashcard 81 – Spanish

Teacher: Est-ce que Carlos est espagnol ou irlandais?
Pupils: Carlos est espagnol.

Teacher: Est-ce que Dolores est espagnole ou irlandaise?
Pupils: Dolores est espagnole.

Ask more questions using the flashcards to introduce more of the nationalities from the *Vocabulary* box.

Vocabulaire

De quelle nationalité est...?	What is the nationality of...?
le garçon	the boy
la fille	the girl

Materials

★ Flashcards 77–81 (pages 224–226)
★ Sheet 8a (page 99)
★ Sheets 8b(i)–8b(ii) (pages 100–101) cut into cards, one set per pair
★ CD, Tracks 21 and 22
★ Photos of famous people of different nationalities, e.g. footballers and other sporting heroes, pop stars, the prime minister, or even cartoon characters such as Astérix, Bart Simpson, etc.

De quelle nationalité est...?

What is the nationality of...?

Using flashcards 77–81 (pages 224–226) or photos of famous people, ask pupils to tell you the nationalities of the different characters represented. Ask the questions to pupils in chorus and then individually, "De quelle nationalité est Phillip?", "De quelle nationalité est Hannah?" etc. You could also use, "De quelle nationalité est le garçon/la fille?" to teach these important words.

Note: The numbers relate to the set of flashcards that can be bought separately

Ask two or three different pupils, "De quelle nationalité es-tu?" waiting for the answer, "Je suis…"

Perform a Mexican wave where every pupil asks the next about his/her nationality, for example:

Zhalore: De quelle nationalité es-tu, John?
John: Je suis anglais.
De quelle nationalité es-tu, Kathryn?
Kathryn: Je suis anglaise.

8a — Ask the pupils to sort the different nationalities into the feminine and masculine forms on Sheet 8a.

8b (i) **8b (ii)** — Ask the pupils to read about famous French people, both past and present on Sheets 8b(i) and 8b(ii).

Play a game in pairs using the cards of the famous French people. Put the cards in a pile, face down. One pupil takes a card without showing it, and their partner has to ask questions in English to try and guess who the person is. You could also get the children to ask simple questions in French, such as "Est-ce qu'il est riche?" or "Est-ce qu'elle est intelligente?"

Track 21 is a dialogue between Monsieur Grand, Madame Petite and Mademoiselle Jolie about nationalities. For Track 22, the pupils will need to answer questions about the nationality of famous personalities in the pauses.

Les drapeaux

Flags

Show pupils pictures of national flags and ask (for example), "De quelle couleur est le drapeau français?" Wait for an answer and then move on to the flag of the next country.

Divide the pupils into groups of four and ask each pupil to write down the name and nationality of a famous person. (If the pupil does not know the nationality or how to say it in French, encourage them to ask you by saying, "Madame/Monsieur, s'il vous plaît, de quelle nationalité est (the famous person's name)?" Answer and encourage the pupils to respond by saying, "Merci Madame/Monsieur." You could reply "De rien!" – "Don't mention it!")

When all the pupils have finished writing down the name and nationality of their famous person, ask all the pupils in one group to stand up. One by one they ask the other groups the nationality of their famous person by saying, "De quelle nationalité est...?" The other groups must each write their answer on a card or piece of spare paper in French, for example, "Il/Elle est français(e)." Then ask one person from each group to hold their group's card up at the same time. The group with the most correct answers at the end is the winner and receives a Tableau d'Honneur.

8c

Ask the pupils to colour in the flags and answer the questions on Sheet 8c. You will need to have reference books and/or access to the Internet available.

Vocabulaire

un drapeau	a flag
De rien!	Don't mention it!

Materials

★ Sheet 8c (page 102)
★ Reference books and/or access to the internet (optional) – type in "national flags" into a search engine to find a wide range of examples, many of which can be printed for free
★ Tableau d'Honneur (page 203)
★ Cards or pieces of spare paper

<table>
<tr><td>

Materials

★ Sheet 8d (page 103)

</td></tr>
</table>

Hexagonie story

Give the pupils Sheet 8d: "Liberté, égalité, fraternité", the next instalment in the Hexagonie story and discuss to reinforce the points covered. You may need to explain that "fraternity" means "brotherhood".

Note

Words which indicate the inhabitants of a town or a country are written with a capital letter, e.g. les Français, but keep a lower case letter when they are adjectives, e.g. Il est français.

<table>
<tr><td>

Materials

★ Sheet 8e (page 104)

</td></tr>
</table>

Essential words and phrases

8e

At the end of this unit, give the pupils Sheet 8e, which will help them to remember essential words and phrases.

Au revoir!

Remember always to wish the pupils a good week or weekend depending on when the lesson takes place. Wait for them to reply "Merci, Madame/Monsieur, vous aussi." Say "À bientôt!" or "À lundi!" (for example).

Nom:_____   **La date:**_____

Trouve et écris

Sort the nationalities from the box below into the correct forms for male and female by writing them in the boxes around the boy and girl.

C'est un garçon…	C'est une fille…

marocain	français	écossaise	chinois	belge	brésilienne
indienne	américain	portugais	portugaise	anglaise	pakistanaise
allemande	belge	irlandaise	française	indien	canadienne
espagnol	écossais	polonaise	italien	polonais	marocaine
brésilien	canadien	américaine	gallois	anglais	galloise
italienne	pakistanais	irlandais	espagnole	allemand	chinoise

One nationality stays the same for both the boy and the girl. Which is this?

_____

For four nationalities an extra "n" is added before the "e". Which are these?

_____

Nom:_____ **La date:**_____

Famous French people

Louis XIV (1638–1715)

Louis XIV was a famous French king who ruled the country for a very long time and who brought art, elegance and good food to the kingdom. He was known as "Le Roi Soleil" ("The Sun King").

Napoléon Bonaparte (1769–1821)

The French Emperor Napoléon Bonaparte was a strong military leader and had plans to invade all of Europe. In paintings of him, he is always shown with his right hand on his heart.

Louis Braille (1809–1852)

When Louis Braille was just three years old he became blind after an accident in his father's workshop. He later invented a system to read using small bumps that the fingers can feel. Today this is used all over the world.

Camille Saint-Saëns (1835–1921)

Saint-Saëns is a famous composer who wrote "Le Carnaval des Animaux" ("The Carnival of the Animals"), with music about a swan, an elephant and even fossils!

Nom:_____   **La date:**_____

Famous French people

Louis (1877–1944), Marcel (1872–1903) and Fernand (1865–1909) Renault

The three Renault brothers founded the French car company Renault in 1899, which now sells cars around the world.

"Coco" Chanel (1883–1971)

Chanel was a famous fashion designer who began by opening a small hat shop in Paris in 1910. Her perfumes are also very famous.

Zinedine Zidane (1972–   )

Zidane is a famous footballer from Marseille. He was captain of the French team "Les Bleus" when they won the 1998 World Cup.

Amélie Mauresmo (1979–   )

Amélie Mauresmo is a professional tennis player who won at Wimbledon in 2006. Bravo, Amélie!

Nom:_____ **La date:**_____

Colorie et réponds

Colour in the flags and answer the questions.

1. De quelle couleur est le drapeau écossais?

   _____

2. De quelle couleur est le drapeau gallois?

   _____

3. De quelle couleur est le drapeau anglais?

   _____

4. De quelle couleur est le drapeau allemand?

   _____

5. De quelle couleur est le drapeau français?

   _____

6. De quelle couleur est le drapeau irlandais?

   _____

7. De quelle couleur est le drapeau belge?

   _____

8. De quelle couleur est le drapeau italien?

   _____

9. De quelle couleur est le drapeau suisse?

   _____

10. De quelle couleur est le drapeau américain?

    _____

Nom:_____   **La date:**_____

Liberté, égalité, fraternité

A very long time ago, the nouns in Hexagonie decided that in their kingdom everyone would be free to do what they wanted and that they would all be considered equal like brothers. So the nouns invented a motto which was

LIBERTÉ, ÉGALITÉ, FRATERNITÉ

which means "liberty, equality, fraternity". This motto became well known throughout the kingdom. It sounded so nice, that soon nouns from all over the world wanted to live there too. Little by little many came.

Obviously, all the nouns born in Hexagonie were "français" and "françaises" while all the others were different nationalities. Every nationality brought something unique that made the kingdom a more interesting place.

The nouns from Italy, called "les Italiens", brought their fashion and their pasta. Those from Spain, "les Espagnols", and from Portugal, "les Portugais", helped to build beautiful new houses. Those from North Africa, "les Algérians", "les Marocains" and "les Tunisiens", brought their religion and their crafts. The Chinese, "les Chinois", introduced their different ways of cooking and their medicine. It would take too long to mention all the different nationalities who lived in Hexagonie. But one thing was sure, Hexagonie became a colourful and interesting kingdom!

Nom:_____   **La date:**_____

Essential words and phrases

How to ask about somebody's nationality

De quelle nationalité…?	What nationality…?
De quelle nationalité es-tu?	What is your nationality?
De quelle nationalité est-il?	What is his nationality?
De quelle nationalité est-elle?	What is her nationality?

How to say "Thank you very much!"

Merci beaucoup!	Thank you very much!
Merci beaucoup, Madame!	Thank you very much, Madam!
Merci beaucoup, Mademoiselle!	Thank you very much, Miss!
Merci beaucoup, Monsieur!	Thank you very much, Sir!

How to reply when someone says "Thank you very much!"

De rien!	Don't mention it!

The plural

Key teaching points/vocabulary
Numbers 11–20
Plural nouns
Animals
The plural article "les"
Use of "des" ("some")
Parts of the body

Bonjour

Say "Bonjour" to the whole class, waiting for the pupils to reply, "Bonjour, Madame/Monsieur." Call the register, and ask at random, "Comment vas-tu?" or "Ça va bien?"

Recap on nationalities

Prepare a list of famous names and ask some pupils about their nationality, for example, "De quelle nationalité est le pape?" "De quelle nationalité est David Beckham?" etc.

Materials
★ List of famous people of different nationalities

Nombres 11–20

Numbers 11–20

Ask the pupils to count to 10, and then say "onze, douze, treize". Encourage the pupils to repeat these three numbers in chorus after you. Then continue with the numbers up to 20.

Perform a Mexican wave from 1 up to 20, and then from 20 back to 1.

Track 23 will help to reinforce the numbers 11–20.

Sing the song, "Un kilomètre à pied" (Track 24 and instrumental version on Track 39):

Un kilomètre à pied,	*One kilometre on foot,*
Ça use, ça use,	*It wears, it wears,*
Un kilomètre à pied,	*One kilometre on foot,*
Ça use les souliers.	*It wears out your shoes.*

Give the pupils Sheet 9a with the words to the song and ask them to join you in singing it.

Once they are familiar with the words to the song, tell them that before each verse you will hold up a card showing a number from 1 to 20, which is the number of kilometres that should be sung. So, for example, if you were to hold up the numeral "2" everyone should sing, "<u>Deux</u> kilomètres à pied."

Vocabulary

onze	eleven
douze	twelve
treize	thirteen
quatorze	fourteen
quinze	fifteen
seize	sixteen
dix-sept	seventeen
dix-huit	eighteen
dix-neuf	nineteen
vingt	twenty
un kilomètre	a kilometre
ça use	it wears
un soulier	a shoe (old fashioned term)
combien font…	how much is…
plus	plus
moins	less/minus

Materials
★ Sheets 9a and 9b (pages 110–111)
★ Cards showing numbers 1–20 written in numerals
★ CD, Tracks 23–25 and 39

Give the pupils Sheet 9b and read the numbers from 1 up to 20. Encourage the children to look for patterns in the way the words are spelt. Point out that the numbers 17–19 are made up of 10 plus a number:

1	un	11	onze
2	**d**eux	12	**d**ouze
3	**t**rois	13	**t**reize
4	**q**uatre	14	**q**uatorze
5	cin**q**	15	**q**uinze
6	**s**ix	16	**s**eize
7	sept	17	dix-sept (10 + 7)
8	huit	18	dix-huit (10 + 8)
9	neuf	19	dix-neuf (10 + 9)
10	dix	20	vingt

Memory trick

The numbers 12–16 all begin with the same letter as the numbers 2–6, except for 15 ("**q**uinze"), which begins with the last letter of 5 ("cin**q**").

Write on the board "5 + 11 = ?" Ask the whole class, "Combien font cinq plus onze?" Encourage the pupils to say in chorus, "Cinq **plus** onze font seize." Do some other addition sums in the same way.

Write on the board "10 – 5 = ?" Ask the whole class, "Combien font dix moins cinq?" Encourage the pupils to say in chorus, "Dix **moins** cinq font cinq." Do some other subtraction sums in the same way. The pupils could now do the sums at the bottom of Sheet 9b.

Track 25 provides oral practice of simple addition and subtraction sums in French. Encourage the children to respond in full sentences.

Play "Loto" (Bingo) by asking each pupil to write 10 different numbers from 1 to 20 on a piece of paper. Call out numbers at random and the winner is the first player to cross out all the numbers on his/her sheet and call out "Loto!"

Materials

★ Sheet 9c (page 112)

Hexagonie story

Give the pupils Sheet 9c: "The nouns club". Read with them this instalment in the Hexagonie story and discuss to reinforce the points covered.

Le pluriel

The plural

Count things in the classroom and write plural phrases on the board, such as "dix cahiers", "sept tables", "dix-neuf chaises", "cinq fenêtres", etc.

Explain that when writing the plural, you add an "s" to the singular noun and that the "s" is not pronounced. However, there are exceptions. When the singular noun ends with "eu" or "eau", you add an "x" to form the plural, e.g. "chapeau" becomes "chapeaux". When the singular noun ends in "al" the ending changes to "aux" in the plural, e.g. "cheval" becomes "chevaux".

Note
If the word already ends in "s" it does not change in the plural, for example "un pays" (a country), "cinq pays".

Les animaux

Animals

Use flashcards showing different animals. Point at one animal on a flashcard and name it, for example, point at a cat and say, "un chat", encouraging the pupils to repeat the word in chorus. Introduce more animals in the same way, always with the pupils repeating the French word after you in chorus.

Point at some animals from the flashcards without saying the French word and wait for the pupils to say it for you.

Note
"Une souris" is an exception to the male/female nouns rule. You might like to ask the children to come up with a memory trick of their own to remember it. For example, girls might think of "Angelina Ballerina".

Ask pupils to mime different animals and the rest of the class has to guess which animal it is and say its name in French.

9d

Ask the pupils to complete Sheet 9d, which reinforces the names of animals and their plurals and provides the pupils with practise writing the numbers up to 20.

Vocabulaire	
un chat	a cat
un chien	a dog
une poule	a chicken
un lapin	a rabbit
une vache	a cow
un hamster	a hamster
un canard	a duck
un cheval	a horse
un cochon	a pig
un cochon d'Inde	a guinea pig
une souris	a mouse
un poisson	a fish
les	the (pl.)

Materials

★ Flashcards of animals listed in Vocabulaire
★ Sheet 9d (page 113)

"Un", "des"

"a", "some"

Tell the pupils that it would be too complicated if we always had to mention the exact number of the things we are referring to. That is why we often use the word "some", which is "des" in French, for example, "some pencils", "some books", "some girls", "some boys".

To remember that the French word for "some" is "des" you could think of the first plural, number 2 ("deux"), as they both begin with "de-".

Vocabulaire	
des	some

Materials

★ Sheets 9e and 9f (pages 114–115)

Stress the fact that nouns and adjectives are both affected by the plural, unlike in English.

Write on the board:

Un garçon intelligent   De**s** garçon**s** intelligent**s**
Une fille intelligente   De**s** fille**s** intelligente**s**

Point out that the adjective has both an "e" and an "s" added for the female plural. Explain that if a word in the singular already ends in "s", such as "français", there is no need to add an extra "s" to form the plural:

Un garçon français   De**s** garçon**s** français

Ask the pupils to write all the phrases on Sheet 9e in the plural.

On Sheet 9f, ask the pupils to read and draw the various items mentioned.

Le corps humain

The human body

Introduce the parts of the body by singing "Head, shoulders, knees and toes" in French: "La tête, les épaules, les genoux, les orteils", pointing at the different parts of your body as they are mentioned. The song appears on Track 26 of the CD. It is sung twice, the second time getting faster. An instrumental version is on Track 40.

Encourage the pupils to join in singing with you until you feel they can remember all the words. At the end of the lesson give every pupil Sheet 9g with the words of the song on it.

Use the cards made from Sheets 9h(i)–9h(ii), or a doll, to introduce more parts of the body.

Note
"Une main" is an exception to the masculine/feminine rule, as it is feminine, although it ends in a consonant.

To play a memory card game, divide the pupils into groups of four and give each group two copies of the cards made from Sheets 9h(i) and 9h(ii). Ask them to place the 15 cards in a pile in the middle of the table, picture side facing up.

Vocabulaire

une tête	a head
un œil (les yeux)	an eye (eyes)
un nez	a nose
une bouche	a mouth
une oreille	an ear
les cheveux (m)	hair
une épaule	a shoulder
un bras	an arm
une main	a hand
un doigt	a finger
une jambe	a leg
un genou (les genoux)	a knee (knees)
un pied	a foot
un orteil	a toe

Materials

★ Sheet 9g (page 116)
★ Sheets 9h(i)–9h(ii) (pages 117–118) photocopied back-to-back and cut into cards, two sets per group
★ Doll (optional)
★ Sheet 9i (page 119)
★ CD, Tracks 26 and 40

To play, each pupil picks up a card in turn, looks at it and says the French word for the part of the body, if they know it. The pupil then checks if his/her word is correct by turning the card over. If it is correct, he/she keeps the card; but if it is incorrect, the card must be placed back at the bottom of the pile. If the pupil thinks that he/she does not know the French word, he/she says, "Je suis désolé(e), je ne sais pas," turns the card over and reads out the French word, then puts the card back at the bottom of the pile. The winner is the pupil who ends up with the most cards.

Draw a stick man on the board and ask a pupil to go to the board by saying, "Va au tableau." Ask him/her to draw a part of the body, saying, for example, "Dessine une oreille, s'il te plaît." Continue with more pupils. At the end of this activity, the stick man will really look funny.

On Sheet 9i, ask the pupils to fill in the blanks with "le", "la", "l' " and "les" in front of the parts of the body.

Essential words and phrases

At the end of this Unit, give the pupils Sheet 9j, which will help them to remember the numbers 1–20.

Materials

★ Sheet 9j (page 120)

Au revoir!

Remember always to wish the pupils a good week or weekend, depending on when the lesson takes place. Wait for them to reply "Merci, Madame/Monsieur, vous aussi!" Say "À bientôt!" or "À mercredi!" (for example). If a pupil wishes you "Bon week-end" or Bonne semaine", reply "toi aussi" which means "you too".

Vocabulaire

| toi aussi | you too (to a friend/child) |

Un kilomètre à pied

One kilometre on foot

Un kilomètre à pied,
Ça use, ça use,
Un kilomètre à pied,
Ça use les souliers.

Deux kilomètres à pied,
Ça use, ça use,
Deux kilomètres à pied,
Ça use les souliers.

Trois kilomètres à pied,
Ça use, ça use,
Trois kilomètres à pied,
Ça use les souliers.

Quatre kilomètres à pied,
Ça use, ça use,
Quatre kilomètres à pied,
Ça use les souliers.

Cinq kilomètres à pied,
Ça use, ça use,
Cinq kilomètres à pied,
Ça use les souliers.

Nom:_____   **La date:**_____

A. Lis

Read

1	un	11	onze
2	**d**eux	12	**d**ouze
3	**t**rois	13	**t**reize
4	**q**uatre	14	**q**uatorze
5	cin**q**	15	**q**uinze
6	**s**ix	16	**s**eize
7	sept	17	dix-sept (10 + 7)
8	huit	18	dix-huit (10 + 8)
9	neuf	19	dix-neuf (10 + 9)
10	dix	20	vingt

B. Écris

Write the answers in words. Say the sums out loud in French.

10 + 8 = _____   19 – 6= _____

11 – 1 = _____   3 + 4 = _____

2 + 10 = _____   5 + 15 = _____

8 + 1 = _____   15 + 2 = _____

20 – 4 = _____   20 – 1 = _____

4 + 4 = _____   10 + 5 = _____

2 + 3 = _____   18 – 12 = _____

7 + 7 = _____   16 – 5 = _____

© Maria Rice-Jones and Brilliant Publications

Nom:_____   **La date:**_____

The nouns club

Every noun in the kingdom belonged to a club where they could meet and play. When they played together they became plural as they were not single anymore.

When two or more nouns were together in the plural, they would add an "s" to their name, for example "livre" became "livres". But if a noun's name already ended in "s", like "ananas" (pineapple) it would remain the same.

Even though the nouns added an "s" to their name in the plural, they still sounded the same, so "banane" and "bananes" sounded the same way as did "coussin" and "coussins".

Seeing all the nouns playing together so happily, another group of words called "adjectives" wanted to join in. They thought that they could add something special, such as the colours of the rainbow, and make the nouns become more exciting!

The nouns liked playing together with the adjectives, so they were happy to let them join their club. When the adjectives and the nouns were together in the plural, they both added an "s" unless they already ended in "s". So, for example, "une pomme verte" became "deux pommes vertes" and "un stylo gris" became "deux stylos gris".

deux pommes vertes

Nom:_____   **La date:**_____

Écris les nombres

Write the correct numbers in words in the spaces.

1. _____ chat _____ chats   2. _____ hamster _____ hamsters

3. _____ chien _____ chiens   4. _____ canard _____ canards

5. _____ lapin _____ lapins   6. _____ cochon _____ cochons

7. _____ vache _____ vaches   8. _____ souris _____ souris

9. _____ poule _____ poules   10. _____ poisson _____ poissons

© Maria Rice-Jones and Brilliant Publications

Nom:_____   **La date:**_____

Écris

Write the following phrases in the plural using "des" and underline the final "s" in all the words.

e.g. une maison blanche   *de<u>s</u> maison<u>s</u> blanche<u>s</u>*

1.   un chat méchant   _____

2.   une poire verte   _____

3.   une vache stupide   _____

4.   un professeur espagnol   _____

5.   un divan rouge   _____

6.   un homme riche   _____

7.   un passeport allemand   _____

8.   un chien intelligent   _____

9.   une banane jaune   _____

10.   un canard brun   _____

11.   une chemise noire   _____

12.   une fille française   _____

Nom:_____   **La date:**_____

Lis 📖   et dessine ✏️

Read and draw

1. trois lapins gris

2. un drapeau français

3. deux tables brunes

4. six poissons oranges

5. une poule brune

6. cinq étoiles jaunes

7. quatre pommes rouges

8. un cochon rose

Nom:_____   **La date:**_____

La tête, les épaules, les genoux, les orteils

Heads, shoulders, knees and toes

La tête, les épaules, les genoux, les orteils.

La tête, les épaules, les genoux, les orteils.

Et les yeux, les oreilles, la bouche et le nez,

La tête, les épaules, les genoux, les orteils.

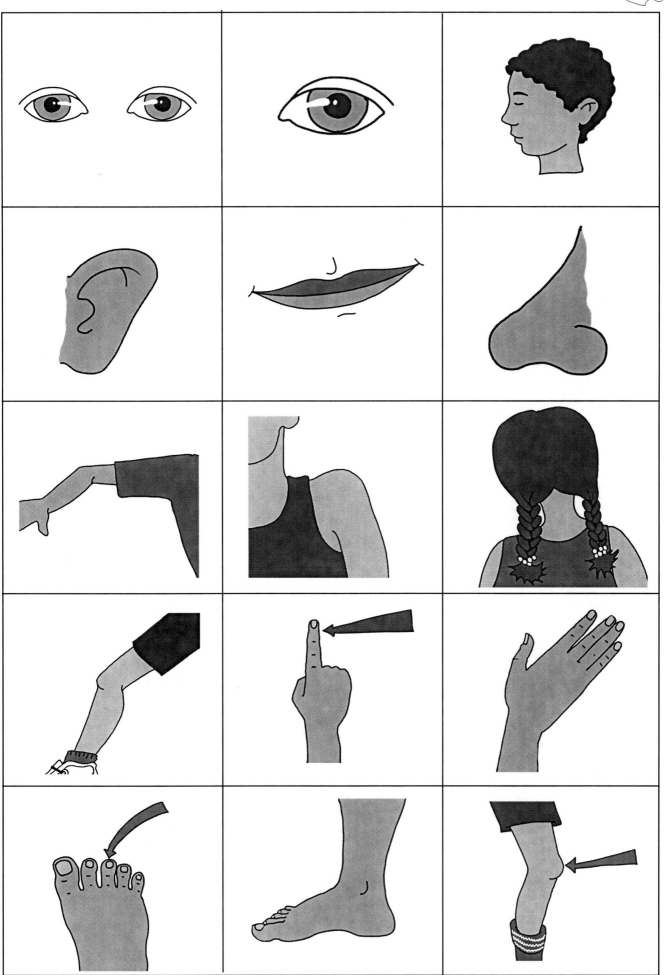

une tête	un œil	les yeux
un nez	une bouche	une oreille
les cheveux	une épaule	un bras
une main	un doigt	une jambe
un genou	un pied	un orteil

Nom:_____   **La date:**_____

Complète

Fill in the gaps using "le", "la", "l'" or "les". Some examples have been done for you.

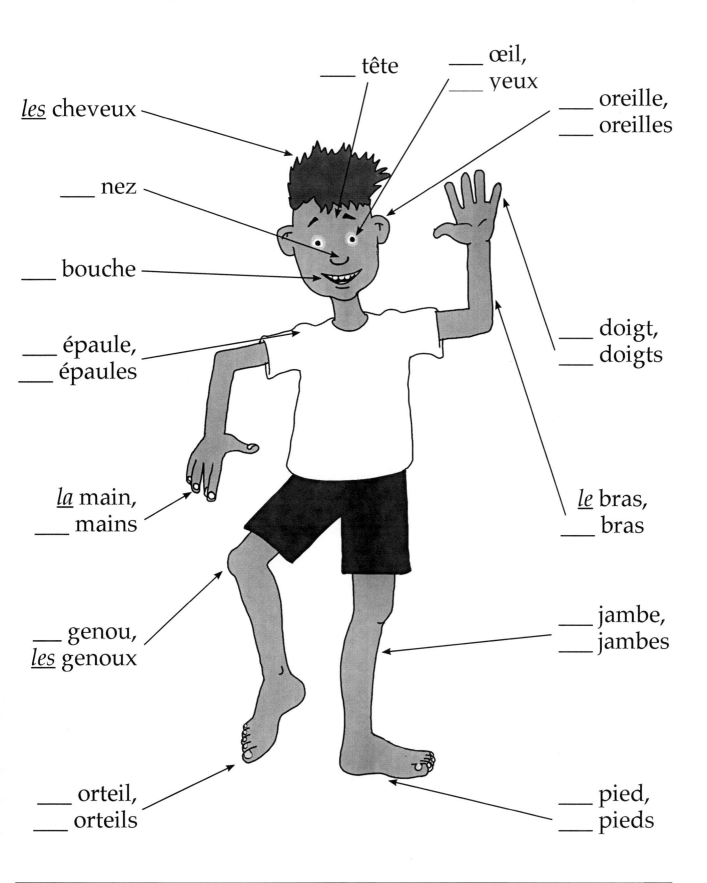

___ tête

___ œil,
___ yeux

___ oreille,
___ oreilles

les cheveux

___ nez

___ bouche

___ épaule,
___ épaules

___ doigt,
___ doigts

la main,
___ mains

le bras,
___ bras

___ genou,
les genoux

___ jambe,
___ jambes

___ orteil,
___ orteils

___ pied,
___ pieds

Nom:_____   **La date:**_____

Essential words and phrases

1	un	11	onze
2	deux	12	douze
3	trois	13	treize
4	quatre	14	quatorze
5	cinq	15	quinze
6	six	16	seize
7	sept	17	dix-sept (10 + 7)
8	huit	18	dix-huit (10 + 8)
9	neuf	19	dix-neuf (10 + 9)
10	dix	20	vingt

What do you have?

Unit 10

Key teaching points/vocabulary

Family members
"Avoir" ("to have") with "je", "tu" and "il/elle"
Sentences with "pas de" ("not any")

Bonjour

Say "Bonjour" to the whole class, waiting for the pupils to reply, "Bonjour, Madame/Monsieur." Call the register, and ask at random, "Comment vas-tu?" or "Ça va bien?"

Recap on "des"

Write singular noun + adjective phrases on the board, such as "un chien intelligent", and ask the pupils to tell you how to make them plural using "des", such as "des chiens intelligents".

Recap on parts of the body and "les"

10a

Tracks 27 & 41

Give the pupils Sheet 10a with the words to the song "Moi, je sais planter les choux."

Moi, je sais planter les choux,
À la mode, à la mode,
Moi, je sais planter les choux,
À la mode de chez nous.
On les plante avec les pieds,
À la mode, à la mode,
On les plante avec les pieds,
À la mode de chez nous.

Me, I know how to plant cabbages,
Like we do, like we do,
Me, I know how to plant cabbages,
Like we do at home.
We plant them with our feet,
Like we do, like we do,
We plant them with our feet,
Like we do at home.

Sing the song and encourage the pupils to join in with you and/or Track 27 on the CD. Sing it lots of times using different parts of the body such as "les mains" or "les doigts". An instrumental version is on Track 41.

Vocabulary

je sais	I know
planter	to plant
les choux	cabbages
à la mode	like we do
à la mode	like we do at
de chez nous	home
on les plante	one plants
	them
avec	with

Materials

★ Sheet 10a (page 128)
★ CD, Tracks 27 and 41

© Maria Rice-Jones and Brilliant Publications

Note:
The original song is "Savez-vous planter les choux?" ("Do you know how to plant cabbages?"). We have changed this to "Moi, je sais planter les choux," because the children will not yet have learned how to conjugate verbs with "vous" at this stage.

Materials

★ Sheet 10b (page 129)

Vocabulaire

un père	a father
une mère	a mother
un frère	a brother
une sœur	a sister
un grand-père	a grandfather
une grand-mère	a grandmother
un beau-père	a step-father/ father-in-law
une belle-mère	a step-mother / mother-in-law
un demi-frère	a half-brother /step-brother
une demi-sœur	a half-sister/ step-sister
j'ai…	I have…

Materials

★ Blank cards for children to write on
★ Tableau d'Honneur (page 203)
★ Stickers (optional)

Hexagonie story

Give the pupils Sheet 10b: "How nice to have Queen Avoir!" Discuss to reinforce the points covered.

La famille

The family

Draw on the board a simple family tree, such as:

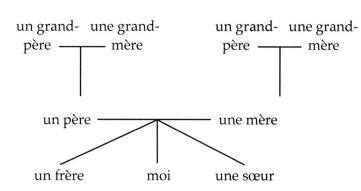

Talk about your family members, e.g. "J'ai trois soeurs et deux frères. J'ai une mère et un père." Ask several children to do the same for their family. You may need to introduce "un beau-père" ("a step-father"), "une belle-mère" ("a step-mother"), "un demi-frère" ("a half-brother/step-brother") and "une demi-sœur" ("a half-sister/ step-sister").

Use "j'ai…" to talk about some of your possessions: "J'ai un stylo rouge." Make sure the children understand that "j'ai…" means "I have…".

Ask the pupils if they can think of a good memory trick for why we say "un" in front of "frère" even though it ends in "e" and why we say "une" in front of "sœur" even though it does not end in "e".

Wait for their answers and tell them that a helpful way to remember is to think of the gender of the family member. "Un" is used for a male person, such as "un père", "un frère", and "une" is used for a female person, such as "une sœur", regardless of the letter these words end in.

Tell the pupils that they are going to play a game called, "Qui suis-je?" ("Who am I?")

To set up the game, ask the pupils to write on a blank card five things that they have or own, like family members or objects, for example, "J'ai une mère française et un père anglais," "J'ai un cahier bleu," etc. Tell them to NOT put their names on the cards. When they have finished, collect all the cards, mix them up and give one at random to each pupil.

To play, one at a time each pupil has to stand up and read what is written on the card that they have been given, and say, "Qui suis-je?" The other pupils have to guess which pupil wrote the card. The winner is whoever has guessed most names correctly. Reward the winner by giving him/her a sticker or a "Tableau d'Honneur".

Description physique

Describing people

Point at your hair, describe it and ask about the pupils' hair individually in the following manner (miming as necessary):

> J'ai les cheveux courts. Et toi, est-ce que tu as les cheveux courts ou longs?

> J'ai les cheveux courts.

> J'ai les cheveux bruns. Et toi, est-ce que tu as les cheveux bruns, blonds ou roux?

> J'ai les cheveux blonds.

Point at your eyes and in a similar way describe them and ask:

> J'ai les yeux bleus. Et toi, est-ce que tu as les yeux bleus, verts ou marron?

> J'ai les yeux verts.

Vocabulaire

les cheveux blonds	blond hair
les cheveux bruns	brown hair
les cheveux roux	red hair
les cheveux longs	long hair
les cheveux courts	short hair
les yeux bleus	blue eyes
les yeux verts	green eyes
les yeux marron	brown eyes

Materials

★ Sheet 10c (page 130)
★ CD, Track 28
★ Spare paper and coloured pencils

Note
You may need to prompt the pupils to say "les cheveux" and "les yeux".
Mention to the pupils that the adjective "marron" is invariable (i.e. it does not take an "s" in the plural) because it is also used as a noun which means "chestnut". It is often used instead of "brun" to describe brown eyes.

Encourage the pupils to ask each other similar questions using, "Est-ce que tu as…?" If necessary, write some prompts on the board for objects they could ask about. For example:

Matt:	Est-ce que tu as les cheveux courts or longs, Jamila?
Jamila:	J'ai les cheveux longs.
Jamila:	Est-ce que tu as un chat, Victoria?
Victoria:	Oui, j'ai un chat.
Victoria:	Est-ce que tu as les cheveux bruns, blonds ou roux, Jack?
Jack:	J'ai les cheveux bruns.
Jack:	Est-ce que tu as un stylo noir, Milán?
Milán:	Oui, j'ai un stylo noir.
Milán:	Est-ce que tu as les yeux marron, verts ou bleus, Tyler?
Tyler:	J'ai les yeux bleus.

Ask the pupils to complete the activity on Sheet 10c either in class or at home.

Give each pupil a spare sheet of paper and some coloured pencils. Ask them to draw pictures of Mademoiselle Jolie, Madame Petite and Monsieur Grand as they are described on Track 28 of the CD.

Vocabulaire

avoir	to have
j'ai	I have
tu as	you have
il a	he has
elle a	she has
j'ai (sept) ans	I am (seven) years old

Materials

★ Sheet 10d (page 131)
★ Toy animal or classroom object

Avoir

To have

Write the French verb "avoir" and the English verb "to have" on the board in the first three persons, highlighting letters in common:

<u>av</u>oir	<u>to have</u>
j'**ai**	I **ha**ve
tu **as**	you **ha**ve
il **a**	he **ha**s
elle **a**	she **ha**s

Ask two or three different pupils their age, saying, "Quel âge as-tu, (pupil's name), sept ans ou huit ans?" waiting for the answer, e.g. "J'ai sept ans."

Hold up Sheet 10d and explain that in French, contrary to English, when we want to say our age we must use the verb "to have", e.g. "J'ai (sept) ans" which literally means, "I have (seven) years. It is as if we "own" our age for one year, and it changes, just like our other possessions sometimes change.

Perform a Mexican wave where the pupils have to introduce themselves and say their age, for example, "Je suis Jessica, je suis anglaise et j'ai huit ans. Et toi?" and "Quel âge as-tu?" Congratulate a good answer with "C'est très bien! Bravo!"

You will need a toy animal or a classroom object for this game. One child leaves the room. The other children take turns to hide the toy on their lap (hidden from view under the table/desk). The first child has to try to find out who has the hidden toy, using "Est-ce que tu as…". For example, if it is a toy cat, the first child would ask, "Est-ce que tu as le chat?" The other pupils should reply with either "Non, je n'ai pas le chat," or "Oui, j'ai le chat." You could limit the number of guesses if necessary. For negative answers, remind them of the memory trick for "ne… pas" (page 82), where the words "ne" and "pas" are like prison walls, that only hold one verb.

10d

Ask the pupils to complete the activity on Sheet 10d.

Autres mots utiles

Other useful words

These words are all things the children might or might not own and have been introduced here, prior to the section on "pas de", to give the children lots of things to talk about!

Use flashcards to introduce the words listed in Vocabulaire. Once you are sure the children are familiar with them, jumble up the cards and pull one out, but don't let them see it. Ask the children to guess which card you have using "Est-ce que tu as…?" Repeat the words in your reply to reinforce them, e.g. "Oui, j'ai un train," or "Non, je n'ai pas de bicyclette." (Using the phrase "pas de" will help the children to get used to this new phrase.)

Note
"Un problème" is an exception to the masculine/feminine rule, as it is masculine, although it ends in an "e".

Vocabulaire

une voiture	a car
une bicyclette	a bicycle
un avion	an aeroplane
un train	a train
un téléphone portable	a mobile phone
des lunettes	some glasses
un parapluie	an umbrella
un problème	a problem
un(e) ami(e)	a friend

Materials
★ Flashcards of items listed in Vocabulaire

Pas de

Not any

Make a series of negative statements with "Je n'ai pas de…" stressing "pas de", for example:

Je n'ai pas de château.
Je n'ai pas de passeport français.
Je n'ai pas de frère.
Je n'ai pas d'avion.
Je n'ai pas d'ordinateur.
Je n'ai pas d'amis espagnols.

Vocabulaire

je n'ai pas de…	I don't have any…

Materials
★ Sheets 10e and 10f (pages 132–133)
★ Tableau d'Honneur (page 203)
★ CD, Track 29

Draw two columns on the board, one for positive sentences and the other for negative sentences, highlighting "pas de" in the negative sentences:

Positive sentences	Negative sentences
J'ai un frère.	Je n'ai <u>pas de</u> frère.
J'ai une sœur.	Je n'ai <u>pas de</u> sœur.
J'ai des problèmes.	Je n'ai <u>pas de</u> problèmes.
J'ai des amis.	Je n'ai <u>pas d'</u>amis.

Point out to the pupils that we do not say "pas un", "pas une" or "pas des", for example it would be incorrect to say, "Je n'ai pas un frère." Instead we use "pas de" in front of a singular noun and a plural noun..

 When a French person "has" or "owns" something, they care about its gender (masculine or feminine) because they are very interested in the things that are theirs. However, for things that do not belong to them, they see no point in indicating the gender. Why bother when it is something that does not belong to them anyway? That is why, instead of using "un", "une" or "des" after "pas", they just use a straightforward "de".

Note
The definite articles ("le", "la", "l' " and "les") are not replaced by "de" in the negative (e.g. "Je n'ai pas les cheveux bruns.")

Ask a series of questions which require negative answers with "je", "tu", "il" and "elle". If you feel your pupils are able, you could ask them to explain why, using "parce que". For example:

Teacher: Est-ce que tu as une voiture?
Pupil: Non, je n'ai pas de voiture (parce que j'ai huit ans).

Teacher: Est-ce que Joanne a un passeport français?
Pupil: Non, elle n'a pas de passeport français (mais il/elle a un passeport britannique).

 Ask a pupil to stand up and think of another pupil in the class without naming him or her. Encourage the rest of the class to ask him/her questions, until they identify who the mystery pupil is. Give a "Tableau d'Honneur" to pupils who do well in asking and answering questions. Here's an example of how the questions and the answers might go.

Question: Est-ce que c'est un garçon ou une fille?
Answer: C'est un garçon.

Question: Est-ce qu'il a un frère ou une sœur?
Answer: Il a deux sœurs mais il n'a pas de frère.

Question: Est-ce qu'il a les cheveux blonds?
Answer: Oui, il a les cheveux blonds.

Question: Est-ce qu'il a les yeux bleus?
Answer: Non, il n'a pas les yeux bleus.

Question: Est-ce qu'il a des lunettes?
Answer: Oui, il a des lunettes.

Question: Est-ce qu'il a un chien?
Answer: Je ne sais pas.

Question: Est-ce qu'il a un chat?
Answer: Oui, il a un chat.

Question: Est-ce que c'est Sam?
Answer: Oui, c'est Sam!

 Ask the children to complete Sheet 10e, which reinforces "pas de" as well as the words for brothers and sisters.

 On Sheet 10f pupils need to answer the questions with "j'ai…" or "je n'ai pas de…".

 On Track 29, the characters use "pas de" while talking to each other about their pets (reinforcing vocabulary introduced in Unit 9). After listening to the track, ask the pupils questions to test their comprehension.

Essential words and phrases

 At the end of this unit, give the pupils Sheet 10g, which will help them to remember essential words and phrases.

Materials
★ Sheet 10g (page 134)

Au revoir!

Remember always to wish the pupils a good week or weekend, depending on when the lesson takes place. Wait for them to reply "Merci, Madame/Monsieur, vous aussi." Say "À bientôt!" or "À jeudi!" (for example).

Nom:_____ **La date:**_____

Moi, je sais planter les choux

Me, I know how to plant cabbages

Moi, je sais planter les choux,

À la mode, à la mode,

Moi, je sais planter les choux,

À la mode de chez nous.

On les plante avec les pieds,

À la mode, à la mode,

On les plante avec les pieds,

À la mode de chez nous.

Nom:_____   **La date:**_____

How nice to have Queen Avoir!

When King Être married his beautiful bride he decided to give her the title, "La Reine Avoir" ("Queen To Have") because he thought she deserved to have everything in life. She already had beauty and grace, and gradually Queen Avoir began to have everything else she wanted too. She liked to have the newest things and the palace was full of them: the latest computers, the latest mobile phones, the latest televisions and so on.

Every noun in the kingdom thought that Queen Avoir was very happy because she had everything. But in reality, just like the rest of the inhabitants of Hexagonie, she had good and bad days. The common mistake made by most of her subjects, the nouns, was to think that the more a person has the happier they become.

But the queen's happiness came from something else. She would often say, "J'ai çi, j'ai ça" ("I have this, I have that") but none of it really mattered to her. What good were all these things to her if she did not share them with others? What made her happy was providing the best for her kingdom and knowing that her subjects did not lack anything they needed.

Nom:_____ **La date:**_____

A. Écris et dessine

Describe yourself using the phrases at the top of the page to help you. In the picture frame either draw or stick a picture of yourself.

les yeux   les yeux bleus   verts les yeux marron

les cheveux   les cheveux   les cheveux blonds   bruns   longs les cheveux   les cheveux roux   courts

C'est moi!

J'ai _____.

J'ai _____.

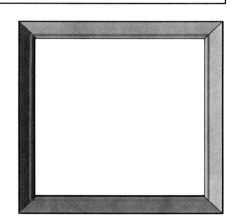

B. Dessine

Draw pictures of Philippe and Nicole to match their descriptions.

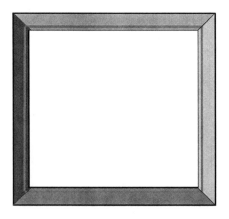

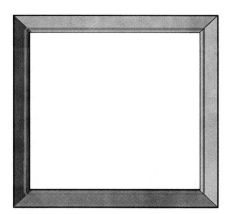

C'est Philippe

Il a les cheveux roux et courts.
Il a les yeux verts.

C'est Nicole

Elle a les cheveux bruns et longs.
Elle a les yeux marron.

Nom:_____   **La date:**_____

Lis et relie

Read and join

J'ai onze ans.

J'ai six ans.

J'ai douze ans.

J'ai huit ans.

J'ai neuf ans.

J'ai sept ans.

Nom:_____ **La date:**_____

Écris

Write how many brothers and sisters each person has. Start each sentence with either "Il / Elle a…" or "Il / Elle n'a pas de…". Write the numbers in words.

For example:

Elle a un frère et deux sœurs.

1.

_____

2.

3.

_____

_____

4.

5.

_____

_____

6.

7.

_____

_____

© Maria Rice-Jones and Brilliant Publications   *This page may be photocopied for use by the purchasing institution only.*

Nom:_____   **La date:**_____

Réponds aux questions suivantes

Answer the following questions with "J'ai…" or "Je n'ai pas de…".

1. Est-ce que tu as un frère?

_____

2. Est-ce que tu as un téléphone portable?

_____

3. Est-ce que tu as un cochon d'Inde?

_____

4. Est-ce que tu as un bateau?

_____

5. Est-ce que tu as un passeport américain?

_____

6. Est-ce que tu as une sœur?

_____

7. Est-ce que tu as des lunettes?

_____

8. Est-ce que tu as un cheval?

_____

9. Est-ce que tu as une Rolls-Royce?

_____

10. Est-ce que tu as des amis français?

_____

Nom:_____   **La date:**_____

Essential words and phrases

How to say "I have a…"

J'ai un…   I have a…

How to say "I don't have any…"

Je n'ai pas de…   I don't have any…

How to say how old you are

J'ai (huit) ans.   I am (eight) years old.

Members of the family

le père (le papa)   the father (the daddy)
la mère (la maman)   the mother (the mummy)
le frère   the brother
la sœur   the sister
le grand-père   the grandfather
la grand-mère   the grandmother
le beau-père   the step-father / father-in-law
la belle-mère   the step-mother / mother-in-law
le demi-frère   the half-brother / step-brother
la demi-sœur   the half-sister / step-sister

Everything is mine!

Key teaching points/vocabulary

Possessives "ma", "mon" and "mes" ("my")

"Bonjour"

Say "Bonjour" to the whole class waiting for the pupils to reply, "Bonjour, Madame/Monsieur." Call the register, and ask at random, "Comment vas-tu?" or "Ça va bien?"

Recap on "j'ai..." and "je n'ai pas de..."

Tell a pupil to ask another pupil of his/her choice a question with "avoir", for example, "Est-ce que tu as un frère ou une sœur?" The other pupil must answer and then ask another question with "avoir" to a pupil of his/her choice, and so on.

Hexagonie story

Give Sheet 11a: "All those possessions" to the pupils. Discuss to reinforce the points covered.

Materials
★ Sheet 11a (page 139)

Les possessifs

Possessives

"Ma"

Point at your chair and say "la chaise" stressing the "**a**" in "l**a**" and say "l**a**, m**a**" making sure that you stress the "**a**". Then say "m**a** chaise" pointing at yourself.

la chaise

ma chaise

Do exactly the same with some more feminine nouns starting with a consonant, such as "l**a** veste, m**a** veste", "l**a** main, m**a** main", "l**a** jupe, m**a** jupe", "l**a** gomme, m**a** gomme", etc.

Vocabulaire

ma	my (+ singular feminine noun starting with a consonant)
mon	my (+ singular masculine noun starting with a consonant or a vowel and singular feminine noun starting with a vowel)
mes	my (+ any plural noun)
maternel(le)	maternal
paternel(le)	paternal

Materials
★ Three blank cards per pupil
★ Sheets 11b–11e (pages 140–143)
★ CD, Tracks 30–31 and 40
★ Spare paper and pencils

Ask the pupils to translate the French word "madame". They should come up with "my dame" or "my lady".

Call out a series of feminine nouns preceded with "la" and starting with a consonant, encouraging the pupils to respond with the same word preceded by "ma", for example:

Teacher:	la voiture
Pupils:	ma voiture
Teacher:	la plante
Pupils:	ma plante

"Mes"

Point at your knees and say "**les** genoux, **mes** genoux". When you say "**les**" and "**mes**" stress the "**es**" so the pupils notice that they both end with the same sound.

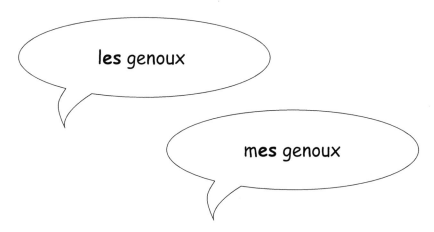

les genoux

mes genoux

Call out a series of plural nouns preceded by "les", encouraging the pupils to respond with the same word preceded by "mes", for example:

Teacher:	les yeux
Pupils:	mes yeux
Teacher:	les épaules
Pupils:	mes épaules

Ask the pupils to translate the French word "mesdames". They should come up with "my dames" or "my ladies".

Memory trick

M**a** comes from L**a**
M**es** comes from L**es**

"Mon"

Ask the pupils to translate the French word "monsieur". They should come up with "my sir". (This is a good opportunity to check pupils' pronunciation of "monsieur".)

From the word "monsieur", it is clear that "my" is said "mon" in front of masculine words in the singular.

Pick up a book, and then say the possessive "mon" in front of "livre" pointing at yourself, "**le** livre, **mon** livre".

Call out a series of masculine words in the singular preceded by "le", encouraging the pupils to respond with the same word preceded by "mon", for example:

Teacher: le nez
Pupils: mon nez
Teacher: le sac
Pupils: mon sac

Now that you have introduced "mon", "ma" and "mes", ask the children to write the three words on blank cards. Call out a series of nouns with "le", "la", or "les" (not with "l' ") such as "le chat", "la chemise", "les poires". The children race to be first to hold up the correct card.

Now sing a variation on the song "Head, shoulders, knees and toes" called "Ma tête, mes épaules, mes genoux, mes orteils" which is on Track 30 of the CD (an instrumental version is on Track 40). The words are on Sheet 11b.

"Mon" + feminine words starting with a vowel

Explain that with feminine words starting with a vowel, such as "épaule", "armoire" and "orange", the French think it sounds clumsy to say "ma épaule", "ma armoire" and "ma orange". Therefore, to make it sound better they use the male possessive "mon épaule", "mon armoire" and "mon orange". However, despite using "mon", these nouns still remain feminine.

The pupils will gradually understand that in French "my" can be said in three different ways depending on what is possessed and not who possesses. This concept will be totally new and can appear tricky for some pupils. This is why you should give lots of oral practice until you are sure that your pupils have mastered the use of "mon", "ma" and "mes".

The article "la" helps us to remember the female possessive "ma" as the "l" is simply replaced by "m", for example:

la mère

ma mère

The article "les" helps us to remember the plural possessive "mes" as the "l" is simply replaced by "m", for example:

les parents

mes parents

For male singular nouns "le" does not help us. But remember that we say "<u>mon</u>sieur" meaning "my sir". That is why we also say "mon" before masculine singular nouns, for example: "mon stylo", "mon père".

Ask the pupils to put "mon", "ma", or "mes" in front of each noun on Sheet 11c.

Ask the pupils to do the activity on Sheet 11d.

Ask the pupils to do the activity on Sheet 11e.

Give each pupil a spare sheet of paper and a pencil. Ask them to listen closely to Track 31 and to draw family trees for Monsieur Grand, Madame Petite and Mademoiselle Jolie. They may need to listen to the track several times. You could look for the regions of France mentioned in the track on a map of France.

Materials

★ Sheet 11f (page 144)

Essential words and phrases

At the end of this unit, give the pupils Sheet 11f, which will help them to remember essential words and phrases.

Au revoir!

Remember always to wish the pupils a good week or weekend, depending on when the lesson takes place. Wait for them to reply "Merci, Madame/Monsieur, vous aussi." Say "À bientôt!" or "À vendredi!" (for example).

Nom:_____   **La date:**_____

All those possessions!

The kingdom of Hexagonie was a place of great freedom and its motto "liberté, égalité, fraternité" worked very well at first. But as time went by, some of the nouns became very selfish and wanted to have more and more things for themselves. They also liked to show off how rich they had become.

So, the nouns began to point at all the things that were theirs and say "my hat", "my book" and so on.

The nouns thought it would be much more impressive to have three words for "my" rather than just one. They came up with "mon", "ma" and "mes". The idea for "mon" came from the word "_mon_sieur" which meant "_my_ sir". "_Ma_" was inspired by the word "_ma_dame" which meant "my lady" and "_mes_" was based on the words "_mes_sieurs" and "_mes_dames" which meant "my sirs" and "my ladies".

When the nouns wanted to show that a feminine thing belonged to them, they would replace the usual "la" with "ma" to show that it was theirs. So "la montre" (the watch) would become "ma montre" (my watch). When they wanted to show that lots of things were theirs, "les" would become "mes". So "les amis" (the friends) became "mes amis" (my friends). "Mon" was always used when the thing that they possessed was either masculine, such as "mon stylo", or began with a vowel, such as "mon uniforme" (my uniform). The inhabitants of Hexagonie thought it sounded so much better to use "mon" with words starting with a vowel, so they used it for both masculine and feminine possessions.

Nom:_____   **La date:**_____

Ma tête, mes épaules, mes genoux, mes orteils

My head, my shoulders, my knees, my toes

Ma tête, mes épaules, mes genoux, mes orteils,

Ma tête, mes épaules, mes genoux, mes orteils,

Et mes yeux, mes oreilles, ma bouche et mon nez,

Ma tête, mes épaules, mes genoux, mes orteils.

© Maria Rice-Jones and Brilliant Publications   *This page may be photocopied for use by the purchasing institution only.*

Nom:_____ **La date:**_____

Écris

Write "ma", "mon" or "mes" in front of each noun.

1. le cadeau

_____ cadeau

2. la chambre

_____ chambre

3. les amis

_____ amis

4. les hamsters

_____ hamsters

5. la mère

_____ mère

6. le pull-over

_____ pull-over

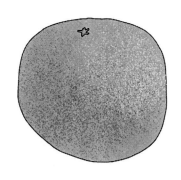

7. l'orange

_____ orange

8. les yeux

_____ yeux

9. le père

_____ père

Nom:_____ **La date:**_____

Complète

Fill in the blanks in the family tree with "mon" or "ma".

Ma famille

moi

___ sœur

___ frère

___ mère

___ père

___ grand-mère
maternelle
(la mère de ma mère)

___ grand-père
maternel
(le père de ma mère)

___ grand-mère
paternelle
(la mère de mon père)

___ grand-père
paternel
(le père de mon père)

Nom:_____   **La date:**_____

Dessine

Draw your family tree. Make it as detailed as possible. Label the people using "mon", "ma" and "mes".

Nom:_____   **La date:**_____

Essential words and phrases

Members of the family

mon père/mon papa	my father/my daddy
ma mère/ma maman	my mother/my mummy
mon beau-père	my step-father
ma belle-mère	my step-mother
mon frère	my brother
ma sœur	my sister
mon demi-frère	my half-brother/step-brother
ma demi-sœur	my half-sister/step-sister
mon grand-père maternel	my maternal grandfather (my mother's father)
mon grand-père paternel	my paternal grandfather (my father's father)
ma grand-mère maternelle	my maternal grandmother (my mother's mother)
ma grand-mère paternelle	my paternal grandmother (my father's mother)
mes grand-parents	my grandparents

Describe with "il y a"

Key teaching points/vocabulary

Phrases using "il y a" ("there is/are")
Types of shop

Bonjour

Say "Bonjour" to the whole class, waiting for the pupils to reply,
"Bonjour, Madame/Monsieur." Call the register, and ask at random,
"Comment vas-tu?" or "Ça va bien?"

Recap on "mon", "ma" and "mes"

Perform a Mexican wave where each pupil says a sentence with
"mon", "ma" or "mes", such as "Mon cahier est grand," or "Ma
mère est française."

Hexagonie story

Give Sheet 12a to the pupils and read: "There is
everything in Hexagonie!" Discuss to reinforce the
points covered.

Materials

★ Sheet 12a (page 150)

Il y a

There is/are

Display flashcard 104 (page 227) depicting a living
room. Point out things in the picture, saying sentences
with the phrase "il y a", for example:

Dans le salon, <u>il y a</u> une petite table.
Sur la petite table, <u>il y a</u> un vase.
Dans le vase, <u>il y a</u> des fleurs.
Dans le salon, <u>il y a</u> une porte.
Sur le mur, <u>il y a</u> un tableau.

Vocabulaire

il y a	there is/are
ici	here
un vase	a vase
Qu'est ce qu'il y a...?	What is there...?

Materials

★ Flashcard 104 (page 227)
★ Small items/miniatures for vocabulary already learnt
★ "Qu'est ce que c'est en français?" (page 200)
★ Bag

Ask the pupils what they think "il y a" means. They will certainly be
able to work out that it means "there is" and "there are".

Ask a series of questions about the classroom with "il y a", first
to the whole class then to pupils individually. You could use the
following examples:

Teacher: Ici (say "here"), est-ce qu'il y a une porte blanche?
Pupils: Oui, ici il y a une porte blanche.

Teacher:	Ici, est-ce qu'il y a des fenêtres?
Pupils:	Oui, ici il y a des fenêtres.

Teacher:	Combien de fenêtres est-ce qu'il y a ici?
Pupils:	Ici, il y a quatre fenêtres.

Teacher:	Combien de tables est-ce qu'il y a ici?
	Combien de professeurs est-ce qu'il y a ici?
	Combien d'élèves (pupils) est-ce qu'il y a ici?

Tell the pupils that you will tell them answers with "il y a" and they have to make up a question for each one, for example:

Teacher:	Il y a deux fenêtres ici.
Pupils:	Combien de fenêtres est-ce qu'il y a ici?

Teacher:	Il y a huit tables ici.
Pupils:	Combien de tables est-ce qu'il y a ici?

 Put in a bag all sorts of things of your choice. Point at it and ask, "Qu'est ce qu'il y a dans le sac?" ("What is there in the bag?") Give the bag to the first pupil, who has to take one thing out of it without looking, and then say, "Dans le sac, il y a...". If the pupil does not know the word in French he/she must say, "Je suis désolé(e), je ne sais pas," and ask the teacher, "Madame/Monsieur, qu'est-ce que c'est en français, s'il vous plaît?" Hold up the sheet with this phrase (page 200) to help them remember it.

Vocabulaire

il n'y a pas de...	there aren't any
un bébé	a baby

Materials

★ Sheets 12b and 12c (pages 151–152)

Il n'y a pas de...

There aren't any...

Say what there isn't in the classroom using "il n'y a pas de...", such as:

> Ici, il n'y a pas de téléphone.

> Ici, il n'y a pas de chat.

> Ici, il n'y a pas de plantes.

Ask questions to the whole class which require a negative answer such as:

Teacher: Combien de voitures est-ce qu'il y a ici?
Pupils: Ici, il n'y a pas de voitures.

Teacher: Combien de vaches est-ce qu'il y a ici?
Pupils: Ici, il n'y a pas de vaches.

Teacher: Combien de bébés (babies) est-ce qu'il y a ici?
Pupils: Ici, il n'y a pas de bébés.

 12b Discuss sheet 12b with the pupils before they attempt it and talk about how "il y a" and "il n'y a pas" look written down. Ask the pupils to answer the questions using these phrases.

 12c Ask the pupils to do Sheet 12c in class or at home. You may wish to revise words for furniture first.

Les magasins

The shops

 Show flashcards showing types of shops one at a time, and for each picture say what it is. Show, for example, the "boulangerie" and say two or three times, "C'est une boulangerie," asking the whole class to repeat. Then ask the whole class, "Est-ce qu'il y a une boulangerie à (the pupils' town)?" If they answer "Oui, il y a une boulangerie," you could ask "Combien de boulangeries est-ce qu'il y a à (the pupils' town)?"

This is an ideal time to talk about how French shops differ from UK shops. Most villages and towns in France still have lots of small specialist shops. Explain the difference between "la pâtisserie" and "la boulangerie" and what you would find in each.

To help the children remember the words, point out similarities with French words they already know, e.g. "poisson" in "poissonnerie" as well as similarities with English words. Encourage pupils to come up with their own memory tricks for remembering the words.

Note
"Le supermarché" is masculine because "é" is not considered to be the same letter as "e".

Vocabulaire

la boulangerie	bakery
la pâtisserie	cake shop
la boucherie	butcher's shop
la poissonnerie	fishmonger's shop
la librairie	bookshop
la papeterie	stationery shop
la pharmacie	chemist
le supermarché	supermarket
excusez-moi	excuse me
près d'ici	near here
juste	just
je ne suis pas d'ici	I am not from here

Materials

★ Flashcards showing types of shops (you could use page 154)
★ Sheets 12d(i)–12d(ii) (pages 153–154) photocopied back-to-back and cut into cards, two sets per group
★ Sheet 12e (page 155)
★ CD, Track 32

Divide the pupils into pairs. Give each pair a set of cards made from Sheets 12d(i) and 12d(ii). Tell them that one pupil will be a passer-by and the other will be a person who is stopping the passer-by to ask if there is a bakery, a supermarket, a bookshop, (and so on) near by. Model the phrase, "Excusez-moi Madame/Monsieur, est-ce qu'il y a … près d'ici?" Encourage the children to use position words in their answers, e.g. "à côté de" and "en face de" (see Unit 7).

The role-play could go as follows:

Abdul: Excusez-moi Madame, est-ce qu'il y a un supermarché près d'ici?

Hannah: Non, il n'y a pas de supermarché près d'ici.

James: Excusez-moi Monsieur, est-ce qu'il y a une librairie près d'ici?

Larry: Oui, Monsieur, il y a une librairie juste en face.

If you feel your pupils are able, you could teach them:

Sara: Excusez-moi Madame, est-ce qu'il y a une boulangerie près d'ici?

Leah: Je suis désolée, Madame, mais je ne suis pas d'ici.

Ask the pupils to do Sheet 12e in class or at home.

Track 32 can be used to reinforce "il y a" and "il n'y a pas de", as well as prepositions.

Vocabulaire

See sheets 12f(i)–12f(iv)

Materials

★ Sheet 12f(i)–12f(iv) (pages 156–159)

★ Maps and guidebooks of Paris (optional)

Visite de Paris

Visit to Paris

In Track 33, Monsieur Grand is showing Madame Petite and Mademoiselle Jolie around Paris by car. The text appears on Sheets 12f(i)–12f(iv), "Visite de Paris." Let the pupils listen to the track first. Although there are many new words, there are enough words that they have already learned or that sound similar to their English equivalents that they should be able to understand most of the track. This should give them a great sense of satisfaction and help to build their confidence.

Afterwards you could go through it again, letting the pupils follow the text on their sheets.

You could extend this activity by encouraging children to find the places mentioned on maps of Paris and in guidebooks.

Essential words and phrases

| 12g |

At the end of this unit, give the pupils Sheet 12g, which will help them to remember essential words and phrases.

Materials

★ Sheet 12g (page 160)

Au revoir!

Remember always to wish the pupils a good week or weekend, depending on when the lesson takes place. Wait for them to reply "Merci, Madame/Monsieur, vous aussi." Say "À bientôt!" or "À mardi!" (for example).

Nom: _____ **La date:** _____

There is everything in Hexagonie!

King Être and Queen Avoir were proud of their kingdom. So proud that they used to say that Hexagonie had everything: "Il y a tout à Hexagonie!"

There were pretty towns with beautiful shops and nice houses, there were big gardens and there were all kinds of entertainment, such as theatres, cinemas and much more.

There was so much in Hexagonie that its inhabitants counted themselves very lucky to live there.

Sometimes the king and queen would try to think if anything was missing in the kingdom: "Qu'est-ce qu'il n'y a pas à Hexagonie?" And if something really was missing they would do their very best to provide it.

Nom:_____   **La date:**_____

Regarde 👁👁 et réponds

Look at the picture and answer the following questions.

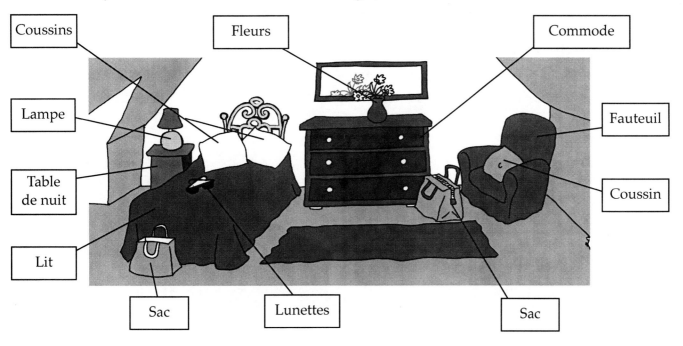

Coussins   Fleurs   Commode   Lampe   Fauteuil   Table de nuit   Coussin   Lit   Sac   Lunettes   Sac

1. Qu'est-ce qu'il y a sur le lit dans la chambre?

    _____

2. Combien de fauteuils est-ce qu'il y a dans la chambre?

    _____

3. Qu'est-ce qu'il y a sur la table de nuit?

    _____

4. Combien de sacs est-ce qu'il y a dans la chambre?

    _____

5. Est-ce qu'il y a un ordinateur dans la chambre?

    _____

6. Qu'est-ce qu'il y a sur le fauteuil?

    _____

7. Qu'est-ce qu'il y a sur la commode?

    _____

8. Est-ce qu'il y a un téléphone dans la chambre?

    _____

Nom:_____   **La date:**_____

Regarde 👀 et écris 📝

Write the correct words from those listed in the box to match each picture.

un divan	des fauteuils	une télévision
un lit	un tableau	des chaises
une armoire	une commode	une table

Dans la salle à manger, il y a

_____ ,

_____

et _____ .

Dans le salon, il y a

_____ ,

_____

et _____ .

Dans la chambre, il y a

_____ ,

_____

et _____ .

la boulangerie	**la pâtisserie**
la boucherie	**la poissonnerie**
la pharmacie	**la papeterie**
le supermarché	**la librairie**

Nom:_____ **La date:**_____

Regarde et relie

Draw lines to match the pictures to the shop where you would find them.

une librairie

une pharmacie

une poissonnerie

une boucherie

un supermarché

une papeterie

une pâtisserie

une boulangerie

© Maria Rice-Jones and Brilliant Publications

Nom:_____   **La date:**_____

Visite de Paris (1)

Visit to Paris

Monsieur Grand: Mes amies, voilà la très célèbre
                    Tour Eiffel. Le créateur de la
                    Tour Eiffel est Monsieur Gustave
                    Eiffel. La Tour Eiffel est le
                    symbole de Paris.

Mademoiselle Jolie: Oh, la Tour Eiffel est très grande.
                    Elle est belle.

Monsieur Grand: Puis voilà le **Pont de l'Alma**. À Paris il y a beaucoup de
                    ponts parce qu'il y a le long fleuve, **La Seine**. Il y a beaucoup
                    de bateaux pour les touristes sur La Seine.

Vocabulaire

célèbre	famous	un symbole	a symbol	un fleuve	a river
une tour	a tower	puis	then	un bateau	a boat
un créateur	a creator	beaucoup de	lots of	des bateaux	some boats
		un pont	a bridge	les touristes	the tourists

Nom:_____ **La date:**_____

Visite de Paris (2)

Visit to Paris

Monsieur Grand: Maintenant, c'est **La Place Charles de Gaulle** avec **L'Arc de Triomphe**. C'est un quartier très élégant avec des boutiques luxueuses, des banques internationales, des restaurants et des cafés élégants.

Mademoiselle Jolie: Et là? Qu'est-ce que c'est?

Monsieur Grand: C'est l'immense **Place de la Concorde** avec **L'Obélisque Égyptien** qui est vraiment magnifique.

Madame Petite: À Paris, est-ce qu'il y a un très grand musée?

Monsieur Grand: Oui, il y a **Le Louvre**. Le Louvre est un très vaste musée d'objets d'art et de tableaux. **La Joconde (Mona Lisa)** de l'artiste italien **Léonard de Vinci** est dans le Louvre.

Madame Petite: La Joconde est vraiment très célèbre.

Vocabulaire

maintenant	now	les banques internationales	international banks	magnifique	magnificent
un quartier	an area	un restaurant	a restaurant	très	very
élégant(e)	elegant	un café	a café	vaste	huge
les boutiques luxueuses	luxurious shops	immense	huge	un musée	a museum
		vraiment	really	un objet d'art	a work of art
				un artiste	an artist

Nom:_____   **La date:**_____

Visite de Paris (3)

Visit to Paris

Monsieur Grand: Maintenant, c'est **L'Opéra Garnier** qui est un splendide palais pour la musique classique et la danse.

Monsieur Grand: Puis le quartier populaire de **Montmartre** avec la grande église **Le Sacré Cœur**. Derrière c'est **La Place du Tertre** où il y a toujours des peintres et des artistes.

Mademoiselle Jolie: Est-ce que c'est un quartier très touristique?

Monsieur Grand: Oui, c'est un quartier extrêmement touristique.

Monsieur Grand: Maintenant, **L'Île de la Cité** dans le centre de Paris. C'est une petite île sur la Seine où il y a la merveilleuse **Cathédrale Notre Dame**. C'est un quartier avec des immeubles très anciens et très élégants.

Vocabulaire

splendide	spendid	populaire	popular	une île	an island
un palais	a palace	une église	a church	merveilleux/	marvellous
la musique	classical	toujours	always	merveilleuse	(m/f)
classique	music	un peintre	a painter	un immeuble	a building
la danse	dance	extrêmement	extremely	ancien(ne)	ancient

Nom:_____   **La date:**_____

Visite de Paris (4)

Visit to Paris

Mademoiselle Jolie: Qu'est ce que c'est là?

Monsieur Grand: Là, c'est **Le Centre Pompidou** qui est un musée extrêmement important pour l'art moderne. Voilà! Le tour est fini.

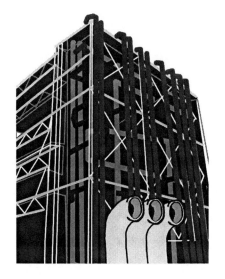

Mademoiselle Jolie: Maintenant je sais que Paris est une ville très jolie.

Madame Petite: Et Paris est vraiment une ville très intéressante.

Monsieur Grand: Oui, Paris est une ville très jolie et intéressante. Vive Paris!

Vocabulaire

moderne	modern	une ville	a city/town	fini	finished
l'art (m)	art	joli(e)	pretty	intéressant(e)	interesting
un tour	tour	aussi	also	Vive…	(Long) live…

Nom:_____ **La date:**_____

Essential words and phrases

How to say "there is/are (not)"

il y a	there is/are
il n'y a pas	there is/are not

How to say "excuse me"

excusez-moi	excuse me

How to ask if something is near by

Excusez-moi Madame/ Monsieur, est-ce qu'il y a … près d'ici?

Excuse me Madam/Sir, is there … near by?

Names of shops

la boulangerie	the bakery
la pâtisserie	the cake shop
la boucherie	the butcher's shop
la poissonnerie	the fishmonger's shop
la librairie	the bookshop
la papeterie	the stationery shop
la pharmacie	the chemist
le supermarché	the supermarket

What matters is to speak

Key teaching points/vocabulary

Possessives "ta", "ton" and "tes" ("your") and "sa", "son" and
    "ses" ("his/her")
"Parler" ("to speak") and "habiter" ("to live") with "je",
    "tu" and "il/elle"
"J'habite en/au/aux/à…" ("I live in…")

Bonjour

Say "Bonjour" to the whole class, waiting for the pupils to reply,
"Bonjour, Madame/Monsieur." Call the register, and ask at random,
"Comment vas-tu?" or "Ça va bien?"

Recap on "il y a"

Ask individual pupils questions with "il y a". For example:

Teacher: Combien d'élèves est-ce qu'il y a ici?
Pupil: Ici, il y a vingt élèves.

Teacher: Qu'est-ce qu'il y a sur la table?
Pupil: Sur la table, il y a des papiers, des livres et des stylos.

Les possessifs

Possessives

"Ton" and "son"

Point at something masculine (such as "un stylo") which belongs
to you and describe its colour, e.g. "Mon stylo est bleu." Point at a
pupil's pen and say, "Mon stylo est bleu. De quelle couleur est ton
stylo?" Wait for the pupil to reply, "Mon stylo est noir." Do the same
with more masculine nouns, such as "un cahier" or "un pantalon".

Ask pupils about male members of their family, for example, "De
quelle nationalité est ton père?" or "Ton frère est gentil (friendly)?"

Ask a pupil a question about the colour of something masculine
(such as "un crayon") that belongs to another pupil. For example:

Teacher: Mon crayon est rouge, ton crayon est orange,
             mais de quelle couleur est le crayon de
             Stéphanie? Est-ce que son crayon est vert ou
             brun?
Isaak: Son crayon est brun.

Do the same with more masculine nouns, such as "un sac" or "un
pull-over".

Vocabulaire

ton	your (+ singular masculine noun starting with a consonant or a vowel and feminine noun starting with a vowel)
son	his/her (+ singular masculine noun starting with a consonant or a vowel and feminine noun starting with a vowel)
ta	your (+ singular feminine noun starting with a consonant)
sa	his/her (+ singular feminine noun starting with a consonant)
tes	your (+ plural noun masculine or feminine)
ses	his/her (+ plural noun, masculine or feminine)

Ask pupils about male members of another pupil's family, for example, "De quelle nationalité est son père?" or "Son frère est grand ou petit?"

"Ta" et "sa"

Point at something feminine (such as "une chaise") which belongs to you and describe its colour, e.g. "Ma chaise est grise." Point at a pupil's chair and say, "Ma chaise est grise. De quelle couleur est ta chaise?" Wait for the pupil to reply, "Ma chaise est jaune." Do the same with more feminine nouns, such as "une jupe" or "une règle".

Ask pupils about female members of their family, for example, "De quelle nationalité est ta grand-mère?" or "Est-ce que ta sœur est gentille?"

Ask a pupil a question about the colour of something feminine (such as "une veste") that belongs to another pupil. For example:

Teacher: Ma veste est brune, ta veste est rose, mais de quelle couleur est la veste de Mario? Est-ce que sa veste est blanche ou bleue?
Siobhan: Sa veste est blanche.

Do the same with more feminine nouns, such as "une gomme" or "une chemise".

Ask pupils about female members of another pupil's family, for example, "De quelle nationalité est sa grand-mère?" or "Est-ce que sa sœur est grande ou petite?"

"Tes"

 Point at some plural objects (both feminine and masculine) which belong to you and describe their colour, e.g. "Mes chaussures sont noires. Mes yeux sont bleus. Mes cheveux sont longs." Write some of these sentences on the board and ask the pupils the meaning of "sont", which means "are".

Now point at a pupil's pair of shoes and say "Mes chaussures sont noires. De quelle couleur sont tes chaussures?" Wait for the pupil to reply, e.g. "mes chaussures sont bleues." Do the same with more plural nouns, such as "les yeux", "les cheveux" etc.

Ask a pupil about plural members of his/her family, e.g. "De quelle nationalité sont tes parents? or "Est-ce que tes grand-parents sont gentils avec toi?" and wait for his/her answer.

"Ses"

Ask a pupil a question about something plural (feminine or masculine) such as "les stylos" which belong to another pupil, e.g:

Teacher: Mes stylos sont verts et tes stylos sont rouges. De quelle couleur sont les stylos de George? Est-ce que ses stylos sont noirs ou ses stylos sont bleus?

Eddie: Ses stylos sont bleus.

Do the same with more plural nouns, such as "les livres", "les chaussures", "les chaussettes" etc.

Ask a pupil about plural members of another pupil's family, e.g. "De quelle nationalité sont les parents de Shanti? De quelle nationalité sont ses parents?" or "Est-ce que ses parents sont ici maintenant?"

 Write the following on the board and point out the similarities between the words. Make sure the pupils understand what they all mean.

the	le (m)	la (f)	les (pl)
	monsieur	madame	messieurs/ mesdames
	my sir	my lady	my sirs/my ladies
my	mon stylo	ma chaise	mes livres
	mon ami		
	mon amie		
	mon hamster		
your	ton stylo	ta chaise	tes livres
	ton ami		
	ton amie		
	ton hamster		
his/ her	son stylo	sa chaise	ses livres
	son ami		
	son amie		
	son hamster		

"Ton" and "son" and feminine words starting with a vowel

Explain that with feminine words starting with a vowel, such as "épaule" and "orange", the French think it sounds clumsy to say "ta épaule", "sa épaule" and "ta orange", "sa orange". Therefore to make it sound better they use the male possessive "ton épaule", "son épaule" and "ton orange", "son orange". However, despite using "ton" and "son", these nouns still remain feminine.

Vocabulaire

parler	to speak
alors	so
une langue	a language
en général	in general
beaucoup	a lot
avec	with
car	because
souvent	often
pourquoi	why

Materials

★ CD, Track 34
★ Sheet 13a (page 169)

Quelles langues parles-tu?

What languages do you speak?

Tell the pupils that they are going to listen twice to Mademoiselle Jolie, whose first name is Julie, talking about herself (Track 34). Ask them to listen very carefully and identify the phrase Julie repeats many times.

After listening twice, the pupils should be able to tell you that Julie says "je parle" many times, and that it means "I speak."

Now listen to the piece again, one or two sentences at a time, asking questions about each.

> **Bonjour, je suis Julie, j'ai quinze ans.**

Teacher: Quel âge a Julie?
Pupils: Elle a 15 ans.

> **Mon père est anglais et ma mère est française. Alors je suis française et anglaise.**

Teacher: De quelle nationalité est son père?
Pupils: Son père est anglais.

Teacher: De quelle nationalité est sa mère?
Pupils: Sa mère est française.

Teacher: De quelle nationalité est Julie?
Pupils: Julie est française et anglaise.

> **Je parle deux langues. Je parle français et anglais.**

Teacher: Combien de langues est-ce que Julie parle?
Pupils: Julie parle deux langues: le français et l'anglais.

> **Je parle anglais avec ma famille et je parle français avec mes amis français.**

Teacher: Quelle langue est-ce que Julie parle avec sa famille?
Pupils: Julie parle anglais avec sa famille.

Teacher: Quelle langue est-ce que Julie parle avec ses amis?
Pupils: Julie parle français avec ses amis français.

> **En général, je parle beaucoup avec ma mère parce qu'elle est gentille avec moi.**

Teacher: Pourquoi est-ce qu'elle parle beaucoup avec sa mère?
Pupils: Parce que sa mère est gentille avec elle.

> **Mais je ne parle pas beaucoup avec mon père car il est très souvent absent.**

Teacher: Est-ce que Julie parle beaucoup avec son père?
Pupils: Non, elle ne parle pas beaucoup avec son père.

 Julie's story is on Sheet 13a. Read it through with the pupils, checking that they understand all the words. Ask the pupils to answer the questions.

Ask individual pupils questions with "tu" and the verb "parler", for example:

> Est-ce que tu parles anglais?
> Oui, je parle anglais.

> Pourquoi est-ce que tu parles anglais?
> Parce que je suis anglais(e).

Ask other questions using "est-ce que" or by putting the verb first and the subject afterwards, such as:

> Combien de langues est-ce que tu parles?
> Combien de langues parles-tu?

> Avec qui est-ce que tu parles français?
> Avec qui parles-tu français?

> En général, est-ce que tu parles beaucoup ou peu?
> En général, parles-tu beaucoup ou peu?

> Avec qui est-ce que tu parles beaucoup?
> Avec qui parles-tu beaucoup?

Note
Explain that the questions mean exactly the same and that both are correct. With some verbs the French feel it is quicker to do the inversion: the verb first and then the subject.

Perform a Mexican wave where the pupils say sentences with "Je parle…", such as, "Je parle français avec Madame/Monsieur (your name)," "Je ne parle pas italien" or "Je parle anglais parce que je suis anglais(e)."

Où habites-tu?

Where do you live?

 Tell the pupils that they are going to listen to Julie again, this time talking about where she lives (Track 35). Ask them to identify the phrase Julie repeats many times.

After listening twice, the pupils should be able to tell you that Julie says "j'habite" many times, and that it means "I live."

Vocabulaire

habiter	to live
exactement	exactly
un appartement	an apartment
le centre	the centre

Materials

★ CD, Track 35
★ Sheet 13b (page 170)

Go through the passage, listening to one sentence at a time, asking questions about each.

> **J'habite en France, à Paris exactement.**

Teacher: Est-ce que Julie habite en France?
Pupils: Oui, Julie habite en France.

> **J'habite avec mes parents et mon jeune frère Matthieu qui a dix ans.**

Teacher: Avec qui est-ce qu'elle habite?
Pupils: Elle habite avec ses parents et son frère.

Teacher: Quel âge a son frère?
Pupils: Son frère a 10 ans.

> **Je n'habite pas dans une maison mais dans un grand appartement dans le centre de Paris.**

Teacher: Est-ce que Julie habite dans une maison ou un appartement?
Pupils: Elle habite dans un appartement.

Teacher: Où est-ce qu'elle habite?
Pupils: Elle habite dans le centre de Paris.

> **Ma grand-mère habite à Nice et ma tante Lucie, la sœur de ma mère, habite à Paris.**

Teacher: Où habite la grand-mère de Julie?
Pupils: Elle habite à Nice.

Teacher: Où habite la tante de Julie?
Pupils: Sa tante habite à Paris.

Ask individual pupils questions with "tu" and the verb "habiter", for example:

> Où est-ce que tu habites?
> Avec qui est-ce que tu habites?
> Est-ce que tu habites dans un appartement ou dans une maison?

Perform a Mexican wave where the pupils ask questions with "habiter". For example, "Est-ce que tu habites avec tes parents?" or "Pourquoi est-ce que tu habites à (name of town)?" The next pupil should answer the question using "habiter", such as, "Oui, j'habite avec mes parents," or "J'habite à (name of town) parce que c'est joli."

The second part of Julie's story is on Sheet 13b. Read it through with the pupils, checking that they understand all the words. Ask the pupils to answer the questions.

Je parle, tu parles

I speak, you speak

Ask some questions orally using "parler" and "habiter", ensuring that you, and the pupils, use "je", "tu" and "il/elle".

Materials

★ Sheets 13c and 13d (pages 171–172)

 Write the following on the board:

je parle	j'habite
tu parles	tu habites
il parle	il habite
elle parle	elle habite

Encourage the pupils to look closely at the way the verbs are spelt. Tell them that there is always an "s" with "tu". Look also at "je" and get them to notice that the "e" is dropped before the "h" in "habite" because it is silent and the next letter is a vowel.

 Ask the pupils to fill in the correct form of "parler" and "habiter" on Sheet 13c.

 Ask the pupils to do the activity on Sheet 13d in class or at home.

Hexagonie story

 Give the pupils Sheet 13e: "The action verbs", the next instalment in the Hexagonie story. Read and discuss to reinforce the points covered. Make sure the pupils understand what a verb is.

Materials

★ Sheet 13e (page 173)

Les pays

Countries

Ask the pupils to look again at Sheet 13c. They will see that there are three words for "in": "en", "au" and "aux". Ask them if they can think of a memory trick to explain why in front of some countries we say "en" and why with certain others we say "au". Then tell them this memory trick:

Vocabulaire

on   one

Materials

★ Sheet 13c (page 171), completed
★ Sheet 13f (page 174)

 When a country ends in "e", you put "en" before it, as "en" also starts with "e", e.g:

en France	in France
en Itali**e**	in Italy
en Angleterr**e**	in England
en Irland**e**	in Ireland
en Allemagn**e**	in Germany
en Espagn**e**	in Spain

When a country ends in a letter other than "e", you say "au", e.g.:

au Pakistan	in Pakistan
au Portugal	in Portugal
au Canada	in Canada
au Japon	in Japan

However, when a country starts with a vowel, regardless of what letter it ends in, you say "en" to ease the pronunciation, e.g:

en Iraq	in Iraq
en Afghanistan	in Afghanistan

When a country is plural and ends in "s", you say "aux", e.g:

aux États-Unis	in the United States

Do Sheet 13f with the pupils. Remind them that "on" means "one" as in the song "Moi, je sais planter les choux".

Les villes

Towns

Tell the pupils that before a town you always say "à":

> J'habite à Londres.
> J'habite à Paris.
> J'habite à Rome.

Perform a Mexican wave where the pupils say where they live, such as, "J'habite à (name of town)," and so on.

Ask the pupils if they have any idea why before a town we must always say "à". Then tell them the following Memory Trick:

Since a town or city is usually smaller than a country, we just put one small letter and use the first letter of the alphabet "à" before it, whereas in front of countries we put a word with more than one letter, "en", "au" or "aux".

Materials

★ Sheet 13g (page 175)

Essential words and phrases

At the end of this unit, give the pupils Sheet 13g, which will help them to remember essential words and phrases.

Au revoir!

Remember always to wish the pupils a good week or weekend, depending on when the lesson takes place. Wait for them to reply "Merci, Madame/Monsieur, vous aussi." Say "À bientôt!" or "À lundi!" (for example).

Nom:_____   **La date:**_____

Lis et réponds aux questions

Read and answer the following questions.

Bonjour, je suis Julie, j'ai quinze ans. Mon père est anglais et ma mère est française. Alors je suis française et anglaise. Je parle deux langues. Je parle français et anglais. Je parle anglais avec ma famille et je parle français avec mes amis français.

En général, je parle beaucoup avec ma mère parce qu'elle est gentille avec moi. Mais je ne parle pas beaucoup avec mon père car il est très souvent absent.

1. De quelle nationalité est Julie?

    _____

2. Quel âge a Julie?

    _____

3. Combien de langues parle Julie?

    _____

4. Quelles langues parle Julie?

    _____

5. Est-ce qu'elle a des amis français?

    _____

Nom:_____ **La date:**_____

Lis et réponds aux questions

Read and answer the following questions.

J'habite en France, à Paris exactement. J'habite avec mes parents et mon jeune frère Matthieu qui a dix ans. Je n'habite pas dans une maison mais dans un grand appartement dans le centre de Paris.

Ma grand-mère habite à Nice et ma tante Lucie, la sœur de ma mère, habite à Paris.

1. Où habite Julie?

    _____

2. Est-ce qu'elle habite dans une maison ou dans un appartement?

    _____

3. Est-ce que Julie a des frères et des sœurs?

    _____

4. Quel âge a Matthieu?

    _____

5. Où habite la grand-mère de Julie?

    _____

Nom:_____   **La date:**_____

Écris

In the following sentences, write "parle" or "parles" in the first space and "habite"
or "habites" in the second space.

1.   Je _____ français

parce que j'_____ en

France.

2. Tu _____ italien parce que tu _____ en Italie.

3. Il _____ espagnol parce qu'il _____ en Espagne.

4. Je _____ anglais parce que j'_____ en Angleterre.

5. Tu _____ allemand parce que tu _____ en Allemagne.

6. Je _____ portugais parce que j'_____ au Portugal.

7. Tu _____ japonais parce que tu _____ au Japon.

8. Elle _____ français parce qu'elle _____ au Canada.

9. Tu _____ chinois parce que tu _____ en Chine.

10. Il _____ anglais parce qu'il _____ aux États-Unis.

Nom:_____   **La date:**_____

Réponds  aux questions

Answer the questions

1. Est-ce que tu parles français à la maison? Pourquoi?

    _____

2. En général, est-ce que tu parles beaucoup ou peu?

    _____

3. Est-ce que tu parles italien? Pourquoi?

    _____

4. Est-ce que tu habites dans une maison ou un appartement?

    _____

5. Est-ce que tu habites dans une ville ou dans un village?

    _____

6. Avec qui est-ce que tu habites?

    _____

Nom:_____   **La date:**_____

The action verbs

In Hexagonie lived another group of inhabitants
called the verbs. The verbs were busy workers whose
actions made it possible for the nouns to do things.

Some verbs were popular like "to laugh" and "to
play". Others weren't very popular like "to cry", "to
suffer" and "to die". Some were naughty like "to
yell", "to scream" or "to misbehave" and some were
kind like the verb "to help".

The verbs belonged to a number of different groups.
The verbs in one of the most popular groups all
ended in "er". "Parler" (to talk) and "habiter" (to
live) belonged to this group. They thought they were
the best group because they were very organized and
most of them followed the same rules.

© Maria Rice-Jones and Brilliant Publications

Nom:_____   **La date:**_____

Lis et complète

Read and fill in the gaps with "en" or "au".

1. On parle français _____ Belgique (Belgium).

2. On parle français _____ Canada (Canada).

3. On parle français _____ Suisse (Switzerland).

4. On parle français _____ Luxembourg (Luxembourg).

5. On parle français _____ Guadeloupe (Guadeloupe).

6. On parle français _____ Maroc (Morocco).

7. On parle français _____ Algérie (Algeria).

8. On parle français _____ Tunisie (Tunisia).

9. On parle français _____ Rwanda (Rwanda).

10. On parle français _____ Cameroun (Cameroon).

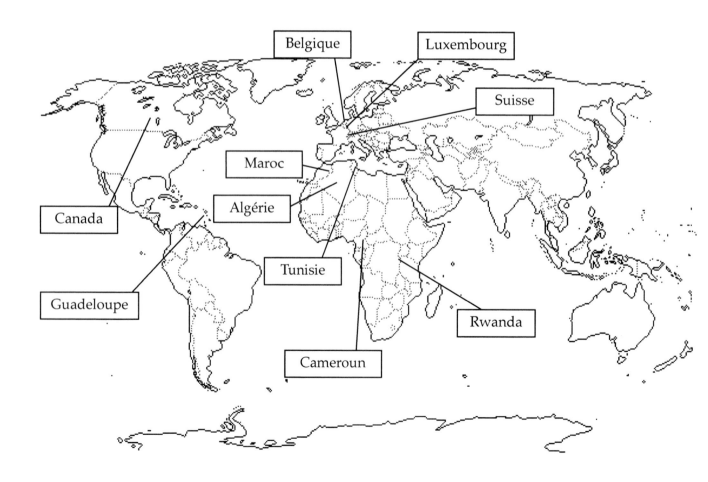

© Maria Rice-Jones and Brilliant Publications   *This page may be photocopied for use by the purchasing institution only.*

Nom:_____   **La date:**_____

Essential words and phrases

Some question words

Où est-ce que…?	Where…?
Pourquoi est-ce que…?	Why…?
Quand est-ce que…?	When…?
Qui est-ce que…?	Who…?
Combien de frères est-ce que…?	How many brothers…?
Combien d'amis est-ce que…?	How many friends…?

How to say "I live in…" (a town or country)

J'habite en…	I live in…	(use with countries ending in "e" and all countries starting with a vowel)
J'habite au…	I live in…	(use with countries that don't end with an "e")
J'habite aux…	I live in…	(use with countries with plural names, such as "les États-Unis" – the United States)
J'habite à…	I live in…	(a town)

Unit 14

Let's study!

Key teaching points/vocabulary

"Étudier" ("to study") and "aimer" ("to like/love") with
   "je", "tu" and "il/elle"
School subjects
Sports
"Je n'aime pas" ("I don't like")

Bonjour

Say "Bonjour" to the whole class, waiting for the pupils to reply, "Bonjour, Madame/Monsieur." Call the register, and ask at random, "Comment vas-tu?" or "Ça va bien?"

Recap on "parler" and "habiter"

Ask individual pupils questions with "parler" and "habiter", such as:

> Est-ce que tu parles anglais?
> Est-ce que tu parles français avec moi?
> Où est-ce que tu habites?
> Avec qui est-ce que tu habites?

Vocabulaire

l'anglais	English
le français	French
les maths	maths
les sciences	science
l'histoire	history
la géographie	geography
le dessin	art
la musique	music
l'informatique	ICT
la technologie	technology
l'espagnol	Spanish
le sport	sport
pendant	during
plaisir	pleasure
à l'école	at school
les matières scolaires	the school subjects
intéressant(e)	interesting
ennuyeux/ ennuyeuse	boring
amusant(e)	funny
difficile	difficult
facile	easy
obligatoire	compulsary
(une) leçon	(a) lesson

J'étudie

I study

Repeat "j'étudie, I study" many times, stressing the common sound at the end of "étu**die**" and "stu**dy**".

 When you are sure that your pupils remember that "I study" is "j'étudie" introduce the words for school lessons. "J'étudie l'anglais", "Est-ce que tu étudies l'anglais?" etc. Flashcards would be useful for this.

Ask questions to the pupils individually, for example:

Teacher:	Qu'est-ce que tu étudies avec moi?
Pupil:	J'étudie le français avec vous.
Teacher:	Qu'est-ce que tu étudies à l'école?
Pupil:	J'étudie l'anglais, les maths, etc.
Teacher:	Est-ce que tu étudies pendant (during) le week-end?
Pupil:	Non, je n'étudie pas pendant le week-end.
Teacher:	Est-ce que tu étudies avec plaisir (pleasure)?
Pupil:	Oui, j'étudie avec plaisir.

Teacher: Quelle est ta matière préférée? (What is your favourite subject?)

Pupil: Ma matière préférée est…

Note
"Une leçon" is an exception to the masculine/feminine rule.

Vocabulaire (cont.)

préféré(e)   favourite
quel(le)   what/which

Materials

★ Flashcards of the school subjects listed in Vocabulaire
★ Sheet 14a (page 179) made into "Cootie Catchers" in advance either by you or the pupils
★ Sheets 14b and 14c (pages 180–181)
★ CD, Track 36

You will need to have several Cootie Catchers (sometimes called a "fortune teller" or a "Chinese counter") made from Sheet 14a. You could give the pupils a copy of the sheet and ask them to make one to bring to the next class.

Divide the pupils into pairs. Pupils take turns at being the Cootie Master who holds the Cootie Catcher and starts the game by asking the other player to choose a number. The Cootie Master then opens and closes the Cootie Catcher that number of times while counting out aloud, "un, deux, trois" etc. When the Cootie Master has stopped counting, the other player must look inside the Cootie Catcher and choose one of the subjects that are shown. The Cootie Master counts how many letters that subject contains and then opens and closes the Cootie Catcher that number of times (so they would open and close it seven times if the subject was "l'anglais", for example). Once the Cootie Master has stopped counting, the player must look at the inside of the Cootie Catcher again and choose a subject. The Cootie Master then flips up the panel with the chosen subject on it, and reads out the question to their partner who has to answer in French.

Ask the pupils to do Sheet 14b in class or at home.

Ask the pupils to do Sheet 14c in class or at home.

On Track 36 Mademoiselle Jolie talks to Madame Petite and Monsieur Grand about what she studies at school.

Vocabulaire

le football	football
le rugby	rugby
le hockey	hockey
le cricket	cricket
le basket	basketball
le baseball	baseball
le tennis	tennis
le golf	golf
la natation	swimming
l'équitation (f)	horse-riding
le ski	skiing
la danse	dance

Materials

★ Sheet 14d (page 182)
★ CD, Track 37

Materials

★ Sheet 14e (page 183)

Est-ce que tu aimes le football?

Do you like football?

Say that in French,"j'aime"' means "I love" or "I like".

Introduce pupils to different sports with questions using "Est-ce que tu aimes…?" while miming various sports. For example:

Teacher: Est-ce que tu aimes le football?
Pupil: Oui, j'aime le football.

Continue until the children are familiar with all the sports and have had lots of practice using "j'aime".

  On Sheet 14d ask the pupils to write about different sports using "J'aime…" and "Je n'aime pas…"

Write a list of sports on the board and ask pupils to write "le", "la" or "l' " in front of each one. They should be able to work them out correctly using the memory tricks they have learned.

Notes

"La natation" and "l'équitation" are feminine, following the memory trick introduced in Unit 5 (page 60).

"Hockey" is a borrowed word from English, so "le" is used instead of "l'"

 On Track 37 Madame Petite, Monsieur Grand and Mademoiselle Jolie talk about their favourite sports.

Essential words and phrases

 At the end of this unit, give the pupils Sheet 14e, which will help them to remember essential words and phrases.

Au revoir!

Remember always to wish the pupils a good week or weekend depending on when the lesson takes place. Wait for them to reply "Merci, Madame/Monsieur, vous aussi." Say "À bientôt!" or "À mercredi!" (for example).

Cootie catcher

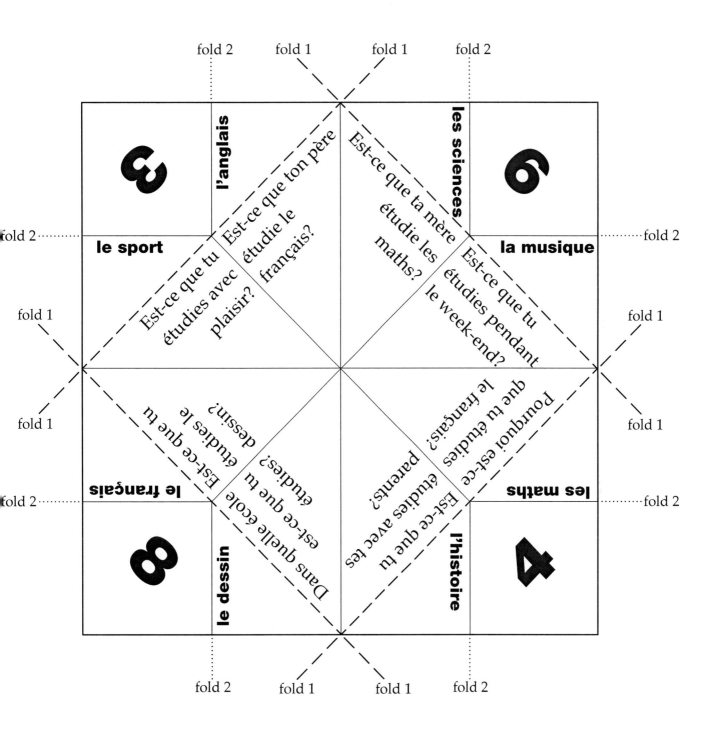

1. Fold corners **back** behind face of paper along fold 1:
2. Fold corners **inward** to centre along fold 2:
3. Put your thumb and forefinger of both hands into the back of the resulting square and pinch up into a point.

Nom:_____ **La date:**_____

Écris

Write about all the subjects you study at school. For each one write some comments. Choose from:

C'est intéressant
(It's interesting)

C'est ennuyeux
(It's boring)

C'est amusant
(It's funny)

C'est difficile
(It's difficult)

C'est facile
(It's easy)

C'est obligatoire
(It's compulsory)

For example: *J'étudie les maths parce que c'est obligatoire.*

_____

_____

_____

_____

_____

_____

_____

_____

Les matières scolaires

(The school subjects)

l'anglais

le français

les maths

les sciences

l'histoire

la géographie

le dessin

la musique

l'informatique

la technologie

l'espagnol

le sport

Nom:_____   **La date:**_____

Réponds aux questions

Answer the questions

1.   Combien de matières est-ce que tu étudies à l'école?

    _____

2.   Est-ce que l'anglais est facile ou difficile?

    _____

3.   Combien de leçons de français as-tu par semaine?

    _____

4.   Quelles langues est-ce que tu étudies?

    _____

5.   Est-ce que tu étudies l'histoire?

    _____

6.   Quelle est ta matière préférée? Pourquoi?

    _____

7.   Avec qui est-ce que tu étudies le français?

    _____

Nom:_____   **La date:**_____

Écris

Write about three sports you like and three sports you dislike using "j'aime…" and "je n'aime pas…".

_____

_____

_____

_____

_____

_____

_____

_____

_____

Les différents sports

(The different sports)

la natation

l'équitation

la danse

le baseball

le hockey

le tennis

le football

le basket

le golf

le ski

le rugby

le cricket

Nom:_____   **La date:**_____

Essential words and phrases

School subjects

l'anglais	English	le dessin	art
le français	French	la musique	music
les maths	maths	l'informatique	ICT
les sciences	science	la technologie	technology
l'histoire	history	l'espagnol	Spanish
la géographie	geography	le sport	sport

How to describe school subjects

c'est intéressant	it's interesting
c'est ennuyeux	it's boring
c'est amusant	it's funny
c'est difficile	it's difficult
c'est facile	it's easy
c'est obligatoire	it's compulsory

Sports

la natation	swimming
le hockey	hockey
le golf	golf
l'équitation	horse-riding
le tennis	tennis
le ski	skiing
la danse	ballet
le football	football
le rugby	rugby
le baseball	baseball
le basket	basketball
le cricket	cricket

Test yourself!

Key teaching points/vocabulary
Review of all the previous units in the book

Bonjour

Say "Bonjour" to the whole class, waiting for the pupils to reply, "Bonjour, Madame/Monsieur." Call the register, and ask at random, "Comment vas-tu?" or "Ça va bien?"

Materials

★ Sheets 15a(i)–15a(iv) (pages 186–189)

Test yourself

Ask the pupils to complete the test on Sheets 15a(i)–15a(iv), which reviews key teaching points from other units.

Guess who?

Ask a pupil to think of another person in the class without saying who it is. The pupil then stands up and the rest of the class ask him/her questions to identify who they are thinking of. Reward pupils who ask good questions, such as:
Est-ce que c'est un garçon ou une fille?
Quel âge a-t-il/-elle?
De quelle nationalité est-il/-elle?
Est-ce qu'il/elle est grand(e) ou petit(e)?
Quelle langue est-ce qu'il/elle parle?
Où est-ce qu'il/elle habite?
Est-ce qu'il/elle a des frères et des sœurs?

Vocabulaire

le prénom	(first) name
le nom	surname
le numéro de téléphone	telephone number
l'adresse	address

Materials

★ Sheet 15b (page 190) cut into cards
★ Sheet 15c (page 191)

New identity

Choose either of these games:

Divide the pupils into teams of four. Give one pupil in each team a card from Sheet 15b, which contains information about an imaginary person. The pupil now takes on this new identity. Give the other three pupils in each team a copy of Sheet 15c, where they will find questions to ask about the imaginary person. Each of the three pupils needs to choose two questions from the list (everyone should choose different questions).

Give the teams a few minutes to prepare their questions and answers before performing in front of the rest of the class. One by one, the three pupils ask the other team-mate, who has taken on the new identity, their questions and wait for his/her reply. Do the same with the other groups. At the end of this activity, you could decide which team has performed the best and reward the members of that team.

Give each pupil one identity card from Sheet 15b, and ask them to imagine they are the person on the card. Give them a few minutes to prepare and introduce themselves to the rest of the class. Do the same with other pupils and at the end reward the pupils who have done well.

Answer a letter in French

Read the letter on Sheet 15d with the pupils and then ask them to answer it.

This letter can also be done as a listening activity, using Track 38.

Vocabulaire

une lettre	a letter
un/une autre	another
pour	for

Materials

★ Sheet 15d (page 192)
★ CD, Track 38

L'école primaire

Divide the pupils into groups of four and ask them to play the game on Sheet 15e, following the instructions. The game could be enlarged to A3 when photocopied.

Vocabulaire

l'arrivée (f)	the finish
Bonne vacances!	Happy holidays!

Materials

★ Sheet 15e (page 193)
★ Dice
★ Counters

Au revoir!

Remember always to wish the pupils a good week or weekend, depending on when the lesson takes place. Wait for them to reply "Merci, Madame/Monsieur, vous aussi." If it is the last lesson before the holidays you could wish them, "Bonnes vacances!"

Nom:_____   **La date:**_____

Réponds ✎ aux questions suivantes

Answer the following questions.

A. "un" or "une"?

Write five masculine words using "un" and five feminine words using "une":

_____   _____

_____   _____

_____   _____

_____   _____

_____   _____

B. "un" or "une"?

1. Tick the correct words:

   Un télévision ☐   une fleur ☐   un maison ☐   une livre ☐
   Une télévision ☐   un fleur ☐   une maison ☐   un livre ☐

2. Think about the story of Hexagonie in "the bad old days". How did this help you to answer B1?

C. Numbers

What are these numbers?

dix-sept _____   quinze _____

douze _____   sept _____

neuf _____   dix _____

six _____   dix-neuf _____

dix-huit _____   cinq _____

Nom:_____   **La date:**_____

D. The colourful kingdom

1. Which letter of the alphabet do most feminine colours have at the end of their name?

2. Give five examples of colours to go with a male noun and five to go with a female noun:

    _____   _____

    _____   _____

    _____   _____

    _____   _____

    _____   _____

E. Asking a question

1. Which expression is used to ask a question in French?

2. In Hexagonie, what is the name given to the officers who always ask questions?

F. "le", "la", "l' " and "les"

Find words to fill the blanks:

le _____   l' _____

le _____   l' _____

le _____   l' _____

la _____   les _____

la _____   les _____

la _____   les _____

Nom:_____ **La date:**_____

G. "être"

1. Translate these phrases into French:

   I am   _____

   You are   _____

   He is   _____

2. In Hexagonie, what is written on the king's throne?

H. "avoir"

1. Translate these phrases into French:

   I have   _____

   You have   _____

   She has   _____

2. Write at least five sentences about things that you have, and at least five sentences about things you don't have.

J'ai un frère et deux sœurs.
J'ai les yeux bleus. J'ai une télévision dans la maison.
Je n'ai pas d'ordinateur.
Je n'ai pas de chien.

Nom:_____   **La date:**_____

I. "mon", "ma" and "mes"

1. Why are there three words for saying "my" in French?

2. Write an example for each:

    mon _____

    ma   _____

    mes _____

J. "parler", "habiter" and "étudier"

1. Write the form of the verb "parler" that is used with "je", "tu" and "il":

    je   _____

    tu   _____

    il   _____

2. Write the form of the verb "habiter" that is used with "je", "tu" and "elle":

    je   _____

    tu   _____

    elle _____

3. Write the form of the verb "étudier" that is used with "je", "tu" and "il":

    je   _____

    tu   _____

    il   _____

Nom:_____   **La date:**_____

Cartes d'identité

Identity cards

Nom:	Way
Prénom:	Rebecca
Pays:	Angleterre
Âge:	17
Adresse:	17 Spring Avenue, Londres
Numéro de téléphone:	0207 643 87 53
Cheveux/yeux:	bruns/marron
Frères/sœurs:	1 frère
Langues:	anglais, espagnol
Sport préféré:	équitation

Nom:	Martinez
Prénom:	Pedro
Pays:	Espagne
Âge:	9
Adresse:	Plaza de España, 1, Madrid
Numéro de téléphone:	921 90 42 10
Cheveux/yeux:	noirs/verts
Frères/sœurs:	3 frères, 2 sœurs
Langues:	espagnol, portugais
Sport préféré:	football

Nom:	Barré
Prénom:	Anne-Hélene
Pays:	France
Âge:	15
Adresse:	25 rue de la République, Nice
Numéro de téléphone:	04 754 42 88
Cheveux/yeux:	blonds/bleus
Frères/sœurs:	0 frère, 0 sœur
Langues:	français, italien
Sport préféré:	tennis

Nom:	Foti
Prénom:	Maddalena
Pays:	Italie
Âge:	12
Adresse:	Via Dora, 2, Milan
Numéro de téléphone:	02 86 35 90
Cheveux/yeux:	roux/bleus
Frères/sœurs:	1 sœur
Langues:	italien, anglais
Sport préféré:	danse

Nom:	Schiffer
Prénom:	Gabriel
Pays:	Allemagne
Âge:	18
Adresse:	Bahnhofstrasse 17, Berlin
Numéro de téléphone:	02 41 38 20
Cheveux/yeux:	roux/bleus
Frères/sœurs:	1 frère
Langues:	allemand, français
Sport préféré:	ski

Nom:	Lenning
Prénom:	James
Pays:	États-Unis
Âge:	6
Adresse:	18 Wall Street, New York
Numéro de téléphone:	583 76 29
Cheveux/yeux:	blonds/verts
Frères/sœurs:	3 frères
Langues:	anglais
Sport préféré:	natation

Nom:_____   **La date:**_____

Questionnaire

Translate the following questions into French then choose two questions to ask the pupil who is pretending to be the imaginary person. Everyone in your group must ask different questions.

1.   What is your surname (nom)?

2.   What is your name (prénom)?

3.   What is your age?

4.   What is your nationality?

5.   What is your address?

6.   What is your telephone number (numéro de téléphone)?

7.   Do you have blond hair, red hair or brown hair?

8.   Which languages (langues) do you speak?

9.   Do you have brothers and sisters?

10.   What is your favourite sport?

Nom:_____ **La date:**_____

Lis et réponds

Read this letter from a French girl called Laura and write a letter back to her.
Remember to answer all of her questions!

Track
●
38

Bonjour,

Je suis Laura et je suis française. Et toi? J'ai huit ans. Et toi, quel âge as-tu?

J'habite à Versailles à côté de Paris. Où est-ce que tu habites? J'habite dans une maison qui a quatre chambres: une chambre pour mes parents, une chambre pour moi, une autre pour ma sœur, Angelina, et une autre pour mon frère, Matthieu. Est-ce que tu habites dans une maison ou un appartement?

Ma sœur a neuf ans et mon petit frère a cinq ans. Est-ce que tu as des frères ou des sœurs?

Je parle un peu anglais parce que j'étudie l'anglais à l'école avec Madame Jones. En général, elle est gentille avec moi. Est-ce que tu étudies le français avec un professeur français?

À bientôt,

Ta correspondante,

Laura

L'école primaire

Nom:_____   **La date:**_____

You need a die per group and a counter per player. Start on "L'école" square, and roll the die to move across the board, answering the questions or following the instructions on the squares you land on. If you cannot do what is asked twice, you are out! The winner is the first player to reach "Arrivée!"

L'école	1. Qui es-tu?	2. Les langues	3. La nationalité	4. L'alphabet	5. Chanson
	Say your name and surname with "I am..." in French.	Quelles langues est-ce que tu parles?	De quelle nationalité es-tu?	Spell your name in French.	Sing a French song with numbers.
11. Chanson	10. Le sport	9. La famille	8. Bad luck!	7. Les nombres	6. L'habitation
Sing the song "Head, shoulders, knees and toes" in French.	Quel est ton sport préféré?	Est-ce que tu as un frère?	Go back to box 3.	Count from 1 to 10 in French.	Où habites-tu?
12. Les nombres	13. Les couleurs	14. Les jours	15. La question	16. Translate!	17. Excuses
Count from 20 to 1 in French.	Say the colours of the French flag, in French.	Say the days of the week in French.	What is needed in French to ask a question?	How do you say, "There is / there are" in French?	Say, "I'm sorry but I don't know" in French.
Arrivée!	22. L'école	21. Les nombres	20. Les animaux	19. Bad luck!	18. Les magasins
	Name five school subjects in French.	Count from 1 to 20 in French.	Say the names of five animals in French.	Go back to box 12.	Name three types of shops in French.

Vocabulary introduced per unit

Unit 1

assiette (f)	plate
au revoir	goodbye
banane (f)	banana
bonjour	hello
bouteille (f)	bottle
bravo	bravo
cahier (m)	notebook
chaise (f)	chair
chocolat (m)	chocolate
couteau (m)	knife
crayon (m)	pencil
cuillère (f)	spoon
et toi?	and you? (to a friend/child)
fenêtre (f)	window
fourchette (f)	fork
gomme (f)	eraser
je ne sais pas	I don't know
je suis…	I am…
je suis désolé(e)	I am sorry
kiwi (m)	kiwi
lampe (f)	lamp
Madame	Mrs/Madam
Mademoiselle	Miss
miroir (m)	mirror
moi	me
Monsieur	Mr/Sir
orange (f)	orange
papier (m)	piece of paper
passeport (m)	passport
plante (f)	plant
porte (f)	door
poster (m)	poster
pull-over (m)	jumper/pullover
pyjama (m)	a pair of pyjamas
règle (f)	ruler
salade (f)	salad
sandwich (m)	sandwich
short (m)	a pair of shorts
stylo (m)	pen
table (f)	table
train (m)	train
très bien	well done
visite (f)	visit

Unit 2

absent(e)	absent
appel (m)	the register
bonne semaine	have a good week
Ça va bien?	How are things?
ça va bien	everything's fine
ceinture (f)	belt
c'est	it is/it's
c'est correct	it's correct
chapeau (m)	hat
chemise (f)	shirt
cravate (f)	tie
jupe (f)	skirt
manteau (m)	coat
merci	thank you
non	no
oui	yes
présent(e)	present
pantalon (m)	pair of trousers
robe (f)	dress
toi aussi	you too (to a friend/child)
veste (f)	jacket
vous aussi	you too (to an adult/group)

Unit 3

armoire (f)	wardrobe
Asseyez-vous!	Sit down!
blanc(he)	white
bleu(e)	blue
bon week-end	have a good weekend
bonne journée	have a good day
brun(e)	brown
bureau (m)	desk
ce n'est pas…	it isn't…
ce n'est pas correct	it's not correct
commode (f)	chest of drawers
coussin (m)	cushion
divan (m)	sofa
fauteuil (m)	armchair
gris(e)	grey
horloge (f)	clock
jaune	yellow
lit (m)	bed
mais	but
noir(e)	black
orange	orange
ordinateur (m)	computer
Qu'est-ce que c'est?	What is it?
rose	pink
rouge	red
s'il vous plaît	please (polite)
tableau (m)	painting
vert(e)	green

Unit 4

aujourd'hui	today
C'est combien, s'il vous plaît?	How much is this, please?
cinq	five
deux	two
dimanche	Sunday
dix	ten
élève (m/f)	pupil
en français	in French
euro(s) (m)	euro(s)
huit	eight
jeudi	Thursday
lundi	Monday
mardi	Tuesday
mercredi	Wednesday
mur (m)	wall
neuf	nine
plafond (m)	ceiling
professeur (m)	teacher
quatre	four
sac (m)	bag
samedi	Saturday
sept	seven
six	six
tableau (m)	(black) board
trois	three
un	one
vendredi	Friday
week-end (m)	weekend
zéro	zero

Unit 5

baguette (f)	baguette
bateau (m)	boat
boulangerie (f)	bakery
cadeau (m)	present
château (m)	castle
Comment vas-tu?	How are you?

comme çi, comme ça	so so
croissant (m)	croissant
dictionnaire (m)	dictionary
fleur (f)	flower
gâteau (m)	cake
je ne vais pas bien	I am not well
je vais bien	I'm fine
je voudrais…	I would like…
livre (m)	book
maison (f)	house
moi aussi	me too
oiseau (m)	bird
pain (m)	loaf of bread
pain au chocolat (m)	pastry with chocolate filling
question (f)	question
télévision (f)	television
Va au tableau!	Go to the board!
voilà	here it is

Unit 6

ananas (m)	pineapple
cave (f)	cellar
cerise (f)	cherry
chambre (f)	bedroom
citron (m)	lemon
cuisine (f)	kitchen
dans	in
De quelle couleur est…?	What colour is…?
école (f)	school
église (f)	church
entrée (f)	entrance hall
étoile (f)	star
grenier (m)	loft (attic)
homme (m)	man
lune (f)	moon
poire (f)	pear
pomme (f)	apple
salle (f)	room
salle à manger (f)	dining room
salle de bains (f)	bathroom
salon (m)	sitting room
s'il te plaît	please (to a friend/child)
soleil (m)	sun

Unit 7

À bientôt!	See you soon!
à côté de	next to
Allemagne (L')	Germany
Belgique (La)	Belgium
bureau (m)	office
capitale (f)	a capital
classe (f)	classroom
dans	in
derrière	behind
devant	in front of
elle	her
elle est	she is
en face de	opposite
Espagne (L')	Spain
Est-ce que…?	*introduces a question*
gentil(le)	nice/friendly
grand(e)	big/tall
il est	he is
intelligent(e)	intelligent
Italie (L')	Italy
jardin (m)	garden
je suis	I am
joli(e)	pretty
laid(e)	ugly
lui	him
Luxembourg (Le)	Luxembourg
Maman	Mummy
méchant(e)	naughty
n'est pas	isn't
ou	or
où	where
Papa	Daddy
parce que	because
pauvre	poor
pays (m)	country
petit(e)	small/short
pourquoi	why
Qu'est-ce qui est…?	What is…?
Qui est…?	Who is…?
Qui suis-je?	Who am I?
riche	rich
sous	under
stupide	stupid
sur	on top of
Suisse (La)	Switzerland
tu es	you are
toi	you

Unit 8

allemand(e)	German
américain(e)	American
anglais(e)	English
belge	Belgian

brésilien(ne)	Brasilian
canadien(ne)	Canadian
chinois(e)	Chinese
De quelle nationalité est…?	What's the nationality of…?
De rien!	Don't mention it!
drapeau (m)	flag
écossais(e)	Scottish
espagnol(e)	Spanish
fille (f)	girl
français(e)	French
gallois(e)	Welsh
garçon (m)	boy
indien(ne)	Indian
irlandais(e)	Irish
italien(ne)	Italian
japonais(e)	Japanese
marocain(e)	Moroccan
pakistanais(e)	Pakistani
polonais(e)	Polish
portugais(e)	Portuguese

Unit 9

bouche (f)	mouth
bras (m)	arm
ça use	it wears
canard (m)	duck
chat (m)	cat
cheval (m)	horse
cheveux (m,pl)	hair
chien (m)	dog
cochon (m)	pig
cochon d'Inde (m)	guinea pig
combien font…	how much is…
des	some
dix-huit	eighteen
dix-neuf	nineteen
dix-sept	seventeen
doigt (m)	finger
douze	twelve
épaule (f)	shoulder
genou (m) (les genoux)	knee (knees)
hamster (m)	hamster
jambe (f)	leg
kilomètre (m)	kilometre
lapin (m)	rabbit
les	the (pl)
main (f)	hand
moins	minus
nez (m)	nose
oeil (m) (les yeux)	eye (eyes)

onze	eleven
oreille (f)	ear
orteil (m)	toe
pied (m)	foot
plus	plus
poisson (m)	fish
poule (f)	chicken
quatorze	fourteen
quinze	fifteen
seize	sixteen
soulier (m)	shoe (old fashioned term)
souris (f)	mouse
tête (f)	head
treize	thirteen
vache (f)	cow
vingt	twenty

Unit 10

à la mode	like we do
ami(e) (m/f)	friend
avec	with
avion (m)	aeroplane
avoir	to have
beau-père (m)	step-father/ father-in-law
belle-mère (f)	step-mother/ mother-in-law
bicyclette (f)	bicycle
blond(e)	blond
(les) choux	(the) cabbages
court(e)	short
de chez nous	at home
demi-frère	half-brother/ step-brother
demi-sœur	half-sister/ half-sister
elle a	she has
frère (m)	brother
grand-père (m)	grandfather
grand-mère (f)	grandmother
il a	he has
j'ai…	I have…
j'ai (sept) ans	I am (seven) years old
je n'ai pas de…	I don't have any…
je sais…	I know…
long(ue)	long
(les) lunettes (f)	(the) glasses
marron (inv)	brown
mère (f)	mother
on les plante	one plants them
parapluie (m)	umbrella
père (m)	father
planter	to plant
problème (m)	problem
roux/rousse	red (used to describe hair)
sœur (f)	sister
téléphone (portable) (m)	(mobile) phone
train (m)	train
tu as	you have
voiture (f)	car

Unit 11

ma	my (+ sing f noun starting with consonant)
maternel(le)	maternal
mes	my (+ any pl noun)
mon	my (+ sing m noun starting with consonant and any sing noun starting with a vowel)
paternel(le)	paternal

Unit 12

bébé (m)	baby
boucherie (f)	butcher's shop
excusez-moi	excuse me
ici	here
il n'y a pas de…	there aren't any…
il y a	there is/are
je ne suis pas d'ici	I am not from here
juste	just
librairie (f)	bookshop
papeterie (f)	stationery shop
pâtisserie (f)	cake shop
pharmacie (f)	chemist
poissonnerie (f)	fishmonger's shop
près d'ici	near here
Qu'est ce qu'il y a…?	What is there…?
supermarché (m)	supermarket
vase (m)	a vase

Unit 12 (Visite de Paris)

ancien(ne)	ancient
art (m)	art
artiste (m)	an artist
banque (f)	bank
bateau(x) (m)	boat(s)
beaucoup de	lots of
boutique (f)	shop
café (m)	café
célèbre	famous
classique	classical
créateur (m)	creator
danse (f)	dance
église (f)	church
élégant(e)	elegant
extrêmement	extremely
fini(e)	finished
fleuve (m)	a river
île (f)	island
immense	huge
immeuble (m)	building
intéressant(e)	interesting
international(e)	international
luxueux/se	luxurious
maintenant	now
magnifique	magnificent
merveilleux/se	marvellous
moderne	modern
musée (m)	museum
musique (f)	music
objet d'art (m)	work of art
palais (m)	palace
peintre (m)	a painter
pont (m)	a bridge
populaire	popular
puis	then
quartier (m)	area
restaurant (m)	restaurant
splendide	spendid
symbole (m)	symbol
toujours	always
tour (f)	tower
tour (m)	tour
touriste (m)	tourist
très	very
vaste	huge
ville (f)	city/town
vive...	(long) live...
vraiment	really

Unit 13

alors	so
appartement (m)	apartment
beaucoup	a lot
car	because
centre (m)	centre
en général	in general
exactement	exactly
habiter	to live
langue (f)	language
on	one
parler	to speak
sa	his/her (+ sing f noun starting with a consonant)
ses	his/her (+ any pl noun)
son	his/her (+ sing m noun starting with a consonant and any sing noun starting with a vowel)
souvent	often
ta	your (+ sing f noun starting with a consonant)
tes	your (+ any pl noun)
ton	your (+ sing m noun starting with a consonant and any sing noun starting with a vowel)

Unit 14

à l'école	at school
amusant(e)	funny
anglais (m)	English
baseball (m)	baseball
basket (m)	basketball
cricket (m)	cricket
danse (f)	dance
dessin (m)	art
difficile	difficult
ennuyeux/se	boring
équitation (f)	horse-riding
espagnol (m)	Spanish
facile	easy
football (m)	football
français (m)	French
géographie (f)	geography
golf (m)	golf
hockey (m)	hockey
histoire (f)	history
informatique (f)	ICT
intéressant(e)	interesting
leçon (m)	lesson
maths (f pl)	maths
matières scolaires (f pl)	school subjects
musique (f)	music
natation (f)	swimming
obligatoire	compulsory
pendant	during
plaisir (m)	pleasure
préféré(e)	favourite
quel(le)	what/which
sciences (f pl)	science
ski (m)	skiing
sport (m)	sport
rugby (m)	rugby
technologie (f)	technology
tennis (m)	tennis

Unit 15

adresse (f)	address
arrivée (f)	finish
Bonne vacances!	Happy holidays!
lettre (f)	letter
nom (m)	surname
numéro de téléphone (m)	telephone number
pour	for
prénom (m)	(first) name
un/une autre	another

Je suis désolé(e), Madame/Monsieur, je ne sais pas.

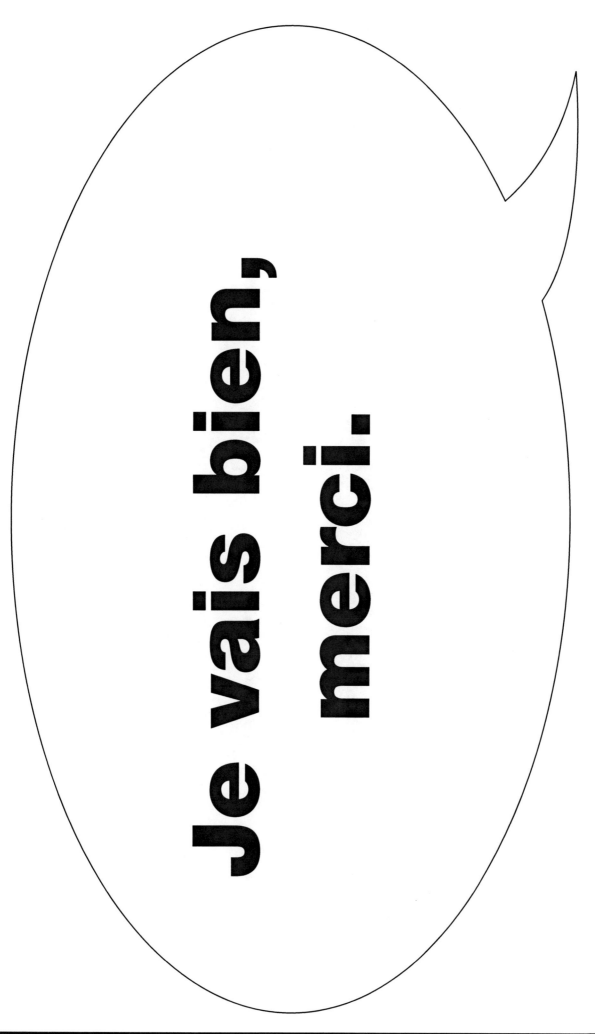

© Maria Rice-Jones and Brilliant Publications

Madame/Monsieur, qu'est ce que c'est en français, s'il vous plaît?

Hexagonie, Part 1

Useful classroom commands

Assieds-toi!

Memory trick: In the French command, there are the same letters as in "sit".

Asseyez-vous!

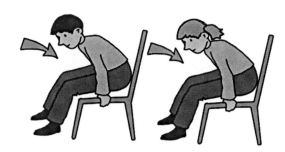

Lève-toi!

Memory trick: The French command reminds us of an "elevator", which goes up.

Levez-vous!

Memory trick: The French command reminds us of an "elevator", which goes up.

Écoute!

Memory trick: The French command reminds us of the word "echo".

Écoutez!

Memory trick: The French command reminds us of the word "echo".

Dessine!

Memory trick: The French command reminds us of the word "design".

Dessinez!

Memory trick: The French command reminds us of the word "design".

Useful classroom commands

Silence!

Memory trick
The French command is the same as in English.

Retourne à ta place!

Memory trick
The French command reminds us of the words "return" and "place"

Répète!

Bonjour!

Memory trick
The French command looks similar to the English word "repeat".

Répétez!

Bonjour! Bonjour!

Memory trick
The French command looks similar to the English word "repeat".

Entre!

Memory trick
The French command is an anagram of the English word "enter".

Entrez!

Memory trick
The French command looks similar to the English word "enter".

Tableau d'Honneur

La date: _____

Nom: _____

Pour: _____

_____
Signature du professeur

Le Roi Être

Madame Petite

© Maria Rice-Jones and Brilliant Publications

Monsieur Grand

Mademoiselle Jolie

© Maria Rice-Jones and Brilliant Publications

Transcript of CD

Track 1

Nar: Hexagonie, Part 1, by Maria Rice-Jones, Copyright Brilliant Publications 2007

Listen to what King Être, le Roi Être, says when he meets three French people for the first time:

Le Roi: Bonjour Mademoiselle!

Mlle Jolie: Bonjour Monsieur!

Le Roi: Je suis le Roi Être. Et toi?

Mlle Jolie: Moi, je suis Mademoiselle Jolie.

Le Roi: Et toi?

M. Grand: Moi, je suis Monsieur Grand.

Le Roi: Et toi?

Mme Petite: Moi, je suis Madame Petite.

✳

Track 2

Nar: You'll need a set of cards made from Sheet 1d. Madame Petite is going to say nine words. She'll repeat each one twice. Listen carefully and hold up the correct card.

Mme Petite: Une fenêtre, une fenêtre
Un stylo, un stylo
Un cahier, un cahier
Une chaise, une chaise
Un papier, un papier
Un crayon, un crayon
Une gomme, une gomme
Une règle, une règle
Une table, une table

✳

Track 3

Nar: Mademoiselle Jolie is going to say five words. She'll repeat each one twice. Draw a picture of each word on a piece of paper.

Mlle Jolie: Une bouteille, une bouteille
Une cuillère, une cuillère
Un couteau, un couteau
Une assiette, une assiette
Une fourchette, une fourchette

✳

Track 4

Nar: Listen to le Roi Être greeting the other characters:

Le Roi: Bonjour Monsieur Grand.

M. Grand: Bonjour Roi Être, ça va bien?

Le Roi: Ça va bien merci, et toi?

M. Grand: Ça va bien merci.

Le Roi: Et Madame Petite, ça va bien?

Mme Petite: Oui, ça va bien merci.

Le Roi: Et Mademoiselle Jolie, ça va bien?

Mlle Jolie: Oui, ça va bien merci.

✳

Track 5

Nar: Listen to this alphabet song, then play it again and try to sing along.

✳

Track 6

Nar: This time some letters are missing from the alphabet song. Sing along, and fill in the missing letters when you hear a gap.

✳

Track 7

Nar: Some different letters are missing from the alphabet song this time. Listen carefully as you sing along. Fill in the missing letters when you hear a gap.

✳

Track 8

Nar: You'll need a copy of Sheet 2c. Look at the first picture. Listen to the question and answer using "C'est" or "Ce n'est pas". Then listen to the response to check if your answer is correct.

Mme Petite: C'est une jupe? Oui, c'est une jupe.

Nar: Now look at picture 2.

M. Grand:	C'est une porte? Non, ce n'est pas une porte. C'est un pantalon.
Nar:	Look at picture 3.
Mme Petite:	C'est une chemise? Oui, c'est une chemise.
Nar:	Look at picture 4.
M. Grand:	C'est un pantalon? Non, ce n'est pas un pantalon. C'est un pull-over.
Nar:	Look at picture 5.
Mme Petite:	C'est un crayon? Non, ce n'est pas un crayon. C'est une veste.
Nar:	Look at picture 6.
Mlle Jolie:	C'est un manteau? Oui, c'est un manteau.
Nar:	Look at picture 7.
Mme Petite:	C'est un pyjama? Non, ce n'est pas un pyjama. C'est une cravate.
Nar:	Look at picture 8.
M. Grand:	C'est un short? Non, ce n'est pas un short. C'est un chapeau.
Nar:	Look at picture 9.
Mme Petite:	C'est une robe? Oui, c'est une robe.
Nar:	And, finally, look at picture 10.
M. Grand:	C'est une chemise? Non, ce n'est pas une chemise. C'est une ceinture.

✻

Track 9

Nar:	Listen to the characters when they say goodbye to each other:
M Grand:	Au revoir Roi Être.
Le Roi:	Au revoir Monsieur Grand. Bonne semaine!
M Grand:	Merci, vous aussi.
Mme Petite:	Au revoir Monsieur Grand.
M. Grand:	Au revoir Madame Petite. Bonne semaine!
Mme Petite:	Merci, vous aussi.
M Grand:	Au revoir Mademoiselle Jolie.
Mlle Jolie	Au revoir Monsieur Grand. Bonne semaine!

M. Grand:	Merci, toi aussi.
Mme Petite:	Au revoir Mademoiselle Jolie.
Mlle Jolie:	Au revoir Madame Petite. Bon week-end!
Mme Petite:	Merci, toi aussi.

✻

Track 10

Nar:	Repeat after Madame Petite each number from zero to ten:
Mme Petite:	0, 1, 2, 3, 4, 5, 6, 7, 8, 9, 10

✻

Nar:	Now, Monsieur Grand and Madame Petite are going to say five series of numbers. In each series, try to find the missing number before the answer is given:
M. Grand:	0, 1, 2, ..., 4. Réponse: trois
Mme Petite:	5, 6, 7, ..., 9. Réponse: huit
M. Grand:	5, ..., 7. Réponse: six
Mme Petite:	10, 9, 8, ..., 6. Réponse: sept
M. Grand:	6, 5,..., 3. Réponse: quatre

✻

Track 11

Nar:	Try to answer these questions before you hear the response.
Mme Petite:	"Monday" en français, c'est lundi ou c'est mardi?
M. Grand:	C'est lundi.
Mme Petite:	"Tuesday" en français, c'est mardi ou c'est mercredi?
Mme Petite:	C'est mardi.
Mme Petite:	"Wednesday" en français, c'est lundi ou c'est mercredi?
Mlle Jolie:	C'est mercredi.
Mme Petite:	"Thursday" en français, c'est mercredi ou c'est jeudi?
M. Grand:	C'est jeudi.
Mme Petite:	"Friday" en français, c'est lundi ou c'est vendredi?
Mme Petite:	C'est vendredi.

Mme Petite:	"Saturday" en français, c'est mardi ou c'est samedi?
Mlle Jolie:	C'est samedi.
Mme Petite:	"Sunday" en français, c'est samedi ou c'est dimanche?
M. Grand:	C'est dimanche.

✱

Track 12

Mme Petite:	"Thursday" en français, c'est lundi?
Mme Petite:	Non, ce n'est pas lundi, mais "Thursday" c'est jeudi.
Mme Petite:	"Sunday" en français, c'est dimanche?
M. Grand:	Oui, c'est dimanche.
Mme Petite:	"Monday" en français, c'est mardi?
Mlle Jolie:	Non, ce n'est pas mardi, mais "Monday" c'est lundi.
Mme Petite:	"Wednesday" en français, c'est jeudi?
Mme Petite:	Non, ce n'est pas jeudi, mais "Wednesday" c'est mercredi.
Mme Petite:	"Friday" en français, c'est vendredi?
M. Grand:	Oui, c'est vendredi.

✱

Track 13

Nar:	Listen to this dialogue that takes place in a clothes shop: "Dans une boutique". You can follow along on Sheet 4f.
M. Grand:	Bonjour Madame!
Mme Petite:	Bonjour Monsieur!
M. Grand:	Qu'est-ce que c'est, s'il vous plaît?
Mme Petite:	C'est une cravate, Monsieur.
M. Grand:	C'est combien, s'il vous plait, Madame?
Mme Petite:	C'est dix euros, Monsieur.
M. Grand:	Merci, Madame.

✱

Track 14

Nar:	Mademoiselle Jolie, Monsieur Grand and Madame Petite are now friends, so they refer to each other as "tu". Listen to how they greet each other.
Mlle Jolie:	Bonjour Monsieur Grand.
M. Grand:	Bonjour Mademoiselle Jolie. Comment vas-tu?
Mlle Jolie:	Je vais bien merci, et toi?
M. Grand:	Moi aussi, je vais bien.
Mlle Jolie:	Bonjour Madame Petite.
Mme Petite:	Bonjour Mademoiselle Jolie.
Mlle Jolie:	Comment vas-tu?
Mme Petite:	Comme çi, comme ça.
Mme Petite:	Bonjour Monsieur Grand, comment vas-tu?
M. Grand:	Maintenant, je ne vais pas bien.
Mme Petite:	Je suis désolée, Monsieur Grand.

✱

Track 15

Nar:	You'll need a copy of Sheet 5a. See if you can answer the questions before the answer is given.
Mme Petite:	Question 1. Qu'est-ce que c'est? C'est un bateau ou un stylo? C'est un bateau.
M. Grand:	Question 2. Qu'est-ce que c'est? C'est un couteau ou un oiseau? C'est un oiseau.
Mme Petite:	Question 3. Qu'est-ce que c'est? C'est un bateau ou un gâteau? C'est un gâteau.
M. Grand:	Question 4. Qu'est-ce que c'est? C'est un château ou un chapeau? C'est un chapeau.
Mme Petite:	Question 5. Qu'est-ce que c'est? C'est un cadeau ou un manteau? C'est un cadeau.
M. Grand:	Question 6. Qu'est-ce que c'est? C'est un château ou un oiseau? C'est un château.

✱

Track 16

Nar:	Listen to these dialogues. They take place in a shop: "Dans un magasin".
Mme Petite:	Bonjour Monsieur!
V1:	Bonjour Madame!
Mme Petite:	Je voudrais un stylo noir s'il vous plaît.
V1:	Voilà Madame!
Mme Petite:	C'est combien, s'il vous plaît?
V1:	C'est 8 euros, Madame.
Mme Petite:	Voilà!
V1:	Merci Madame, et au revoir.
Mme Petite:	Au revoir Monsieur et merci.

✳

Mme Petite:	Bonjour Monsieur!
V1:	Bonjour Madame!
Mme Petite:	Je voudrais un pyjama bleu s'il vous plaît.
V1:	Voilà Madame!
Mme Petite:	C'est combien, s'il vous plaît?
V1:	C'est 10 euros, Madame.
Mme Petite:	Voilà!
V1:	Merci Madame et au revoir.
Mme Petite:	Au revoir Monsieur et merci.

✳

M. Grand:	Bonjour Mademoiselle!
V1:	Bonjour Monsieur!
M. Grand:	Je voudrais une baguette, s'il vous plaît.
V1:	Voilà!
M. Grand:	C'est combien, s'il vous plaît?
V1:	C'est un euro Monsieur.
M. Grand:	Voilà!
V1:	Merci Monsieur. Au revoir Monsieur!
M. Grand:	Merci Mademoiselle. Au revoir!

✳

Track 17

Nar:	Look at the flashcards your teacher holds up and answer the questions. Then check if your answers are correct. Flashcard 61.
Mme Petite:	C'est le salon ou la salon? C'est le salon.
Nar:	Flashcard 62.
M. Grand:	C'est le salon ou la cuisine? Ce n'est pas le salon mais c'est la cuisine.
Nar:	Flashcard 63.
Mme Petite:	C'est le salle à manger ou la salle à manger? C'est la salle à manger.
Nar:	Flashcard 64.
M. Grand:	C'est l'entrée ou la salle de bains? Ce n'est pas la salle de bains mais c'est l'entrée.
Nar:	Flashcard 65.
Mme Petite:	C'est la cave ou le cave? C'est la cave.
Nar:	Flashcard 66.
M. Grand:	C'est le grenier ou la grenier? C'est le grenier.
Nar:	Flashcard 67.
Mme Petite:	C'est le chambre ou la chambre? C'est la chambre.
Nar:	Flashcard 68.
M. Grand:	C'est la cuisine ou la salle de bains? Ce n'est pas la cuisine mais c'est la salle de bains.

✳

Track 18

Le Roi:	In my kingdom, I like everything to be bright and colourful. I especially like fruit as they come in so many colours. I hope you know the colours of my favourite fruit. Let's do a quiz: De quelle couleur est le citron?
Mme Petite:	Le citron est jaune.
Le Roi:	C'est correct, Madame Petite, le citron est jaune. De quelle couleur est l'orange?

M. Grand:	L'orange est orange.
Le Roi:	Oui, Monsieur Grand, l'orange est orange.
	De quelle couleur est la banane?
Mlle Jolie:	La banane est jaune.
Le Roi:	Très bien, Mademoiselle Jolie, la banane est jaune.
	De quelle couleur est le kiwi?
Mme Petite:	Le kiwi est vert.
Le Roi:	Bravo, Madame Petite! Le kiwi est vert.
	De quelle couleur est la cerise?
M. Grand:	La cerise est rouge.
Le Roi:	C'est correct Monsieur Grand. La cerise est rouge. Bravo!

✳

Track 19

Nar:	Listen to this track and then answer the questions.
Mme Petite:	Est-ce que Monsieur Grand est petit? Non, Monsieur Grand n'est pas petit parce que Monsieur Grand est grand.
M. Grand:	Est-ce que Madame Petite est grande? Non, Madame Petite n'est pas grande parce que Madame Petite est petite.
Nar:	What will a short boy answer when asked the following question:
Mme Petite:	Est-ce que tu es grand ou petit?
Nar:	He'll answer:
M. Grand:	Je suis petit.
Nar:	Now, what will a tall girl answer when asked the following question:
Mlle Jolie:	Est-ce que tu es grande ou petite?
Nar:	She'll answer:
Mme Petite:	Je suis grande.

✳

Track 20

Nar:	Look at Sheet 7g and answer the following questions. I'm going to give you an example. Example: Julie est devant moi. Qui suis-je? Je suis Daniel.
Mme Petite:	Question 1: Henri est derrière moi. Qui suis-je? Je suis Hélène.
M. Grand:	Question 2: Anne est à côté de moi. Qui suis-je? Je suis Henri.
Mlle Jolie:	Question 3: Henri est à côté de moi et Aurélie est devant moi. Qui suis-je? Je suis Anne.
M. Grand:	Question 4: Le professeur est en face de moi. Qui suis-je? Je suis Luc.
Mlle Jolie:	Question 5: Christophe est devant moi et Anne est derrière moi. Qui suis-je? Je suis Aurélie.
Le Roi:	Question 6: Luc est à coté de moi et Julie est derrière moi. Qui suis-je? Je suis Jean-Pierre.
Mme Petite:	Question 7: Hélène est à côté de moi et Jean-Pierre est devant moi. Qui suis-je? Je suis Julie.
M. Grand:	Question 8: Luc est à côté de moi et Aurélie est derrière moi. Qui suis-je? Je suis Christophe.

✳

Track 21

Nar:	Listen to Monsieur Grand, Madame Petite and Mademoiselle Jolie talking about different people's nationalities. See if you can respond before the answer is given.
M. Grand:	De quelle nationalité es-tu?
Mme Petite:	Je suis française. Et toi, de quelle nationalité es-tu?
M. Grand:	Je suis français aussi.
Mlle Jolie:	De quelle nationalité est Monsieur Grand?
Mme Petite:	Il est français.
Mlle Jolie:	De quelle nationalité est Madame Petite?
M. Grand:	Elle est française.

Mme Petite:	De quelle nationalité est Harry Potter?
M. Grand:	Il est anglais.
Mlle Jolie:	De quelle nationalité est la reine Elizabeth II?
Mme Petite:	Elle est anglaise.
Nar:	Now, what will an English boy answer when asked the following question: Est-ce que tu es français? He will answer:
M. Grand:	Non, je ne suis pas français, je suis anglais.
Nar:	What will an English girl answer when asked the following question: Est-ce que tu es française? She will answer:
Mlle Jolie:	Non, je ne suis pas française, je suis anglaise.

✶

Track 22

Nar:	Try to answer these questions :
Mme Petite:	Est-ce que le Président de la France est italien?
Mme Petite:	Non, le Président de la France n'est pas italien, mais il est français.
Mlle Jolie:	Est-ce qu' Astérix est américain? Non, Astérix n'est pas américain, mais il est français.
M. Grand:	Est-ce que Madame Petite est chinoise? Non, Madame Petite n'est pas chinoise, mais elle est française.
Le Roi:	Est-ce que Mademoiselle Jolie est allemande? Non, Mademoiselle Jolie n'est pas allemande, mais elle est française.

✶

Track 23

Nar:	Repeat after Monsieur Grand each number from ten to twenty:
M. Grand:	10, 11, 12, 13, 14, 15, 16, 17, 18, 19, 20
Nar:	Now repeat after le Roi Être each number from twenty to ten.

Le Roi:	20, 19, 18, 17, 16, 15, 14, 13, 12, 11, 10
Nar:	Now Madame Petite and Monsieur Grand are going to say five series of numbers. In each series, find the missing number:
Mme Petite:	10, 11, 12, ..., 14. Réponse: treize
M. Grand:	15, 16, 17, ..., 19. Réponse: dix-huit
Mme Petite:	15, ..., 17. Réponse: seize
M. Grand:	20, 19, 18, ..., 16. Réponse: dix-sept
Mme Petite:	16, 15, ..., 13. Réponse: quatorze

✶

Track 24

Nar:	Listen to this famous song that French children sing when they are out walking. The song includes the numbers from 1 to 5. Continue with your teacher's help.

✶

Track 25

Nar:	Listen to these adding up sums. Can you work out the answer before it's given?
Mme Petite:	Combien font dix plus sept?
Mlle Jolie:	Dix plus sept font dix-sept.
Mme Petite:	Très bien. Combien font onze plus deux?
M. Grand:	Onze plus deux font treize.
Mme Petite:	Bravo! Combien font sept plus huit?
Mlle Jolie:	Sept plus huit font quinze.
Mme Petite:	Oui, c'est correct. Combien font douze plus six?
M. Grand:	Douze plus six font dix-huit.
Mme Petite:	Très bien. Combien font dix plus dix?
Mlle Jolie:	Dix plus dix font vingt.
Mme Petite:	C'est exact. Bravo!

✶

Narrator:	Now try these subtraction sums.
Mme Petite:	Combien font dix-neuf moins dix?
M. Grand:	Dix-neuf moins dix font neuf.

Mme Petite:	Excellent! Combien font treize moins quatre?
Mlle Jolie:	Treize moins quatre font neuf.
Mme Petite:	Très bien. Combien font dix moins sept?
M. Grand:	Dix moins sept font trois.
Mme Petite:	Bravo! Combien font vingt moins quinze?
Mlle Jolie:	Vingt moins quinze font cinq.
Mme Petite:	Oui, c'est correct. Combien font neuf moins trois?
M. Grand:	Neuf moins trois font cinq.
Mme Petite:	Non, je suis désolée, mais ce n'est pas correct. Je répète. Combien font neuf moins trois?
M. Grand:	Neuf moins trois font six.
Mme Petite:	Bravo! C'est correct.

*

Track 26

Narrator:	Listen to this famous song, then sing along.

*

Track 27

Nar:	Listen to this famous French song and then sing along with it. With your teacher's help, continue singing the song but replace 'les pieds' with another part of the body. For example: les mains, les doigts, etc.

*

Track 28

Nar:	Listen to the descriptions of Monsieur Grand, Madame Petite and Mademoiselle Jolie and draw them on a piece of paper:
Le Roi:	Mademoiselle Jolie a les cheveux longs.
	Elle a les cheveux bruns.
	Elle a les yeux bleus.
Le Roi:	Madame Petite a les cheveux courts.
	Elle a les cheveux blonds.
	Elle a les yeux verts.

Le Roi:	Monsieur Grand a les cheveux courts.
	Il a les cheveux roux.
	Il a les yeux marron.

Track 29

Nar:	Listen carefully to Mademoiselle Jolie, Monsieur Grand and Madame Petite talking about their pets. Pay attention as afterwards your teacher will ask you questions!
Mlle Jolie:	Madame Petite, est-ce que tu as un chat?
Mme Petite:	Oui, j'ai un chat. Et toi?
Mlle Jolie:	Non, moi, je n'ai pas de chat, mais j'ai un chien.
	Monsieur Grand, est-ce que tu as un chat?
M. Grand:	Non, je n'ai pas de chat.
Mme Petite:	Est-ce que tu as un chien?
M. Grand:	Non, je n'ai pas d'animal.

*

Track 30

Nar:	Listen to this song and then sing along with it.

*

Track 31

Nar:	Our friends, Monsieur Grand, Madame Petite and Mademoiselle Jolie, are going to talk about their families. Draw a family tree for each one of them.
M. Grand:	Mon père Jean est parisien mais ma mère Maria est italienne. Ma soeur Émilie est petite et blonde.

*

Mme Petite:	Mon père Victor est normand et ma mère Christine est normande aussi. Je n'ai pas de frères et je n'ai pas de sœurs.

*

Mlle Jolie:	Mon père Alan est breton et ma mère Sylvie est parisienne. Mon petit frère Matthieu est blond.

Track 32

Mme Petite:	Excusez-moi Monsieur, est-ce qu'il y a une boulangerie près d'ici?
M. Grand:	Oui, il y a une boulangerie près d'ici.
Mlle Jolie:	Excusez-moi Madame, est-ce qu'il y a une pâtisserie près d'ici?
Mme Petite:	Non, il n'y a pas de pâtisserie près d'ici.
M. Grand:	Excusez-moi Mademoiselle, est-ce qu'il y a une librairie près d'ici?
Mlle Jolie:	Oui, Monsieur, il y a une librairie juste en face.

Track 33

Nar:	Monsieur Grand is showing Madame Petite and Mademoiselle Jolie around Paris by car.
M. Grand:	Mes amies, voilà la très célèbre Tour Eiffel. Le créateur de la Tour Eiffel est Monsieur Gustave Eiffel. La Tour Eiffel est le symbole de Paris.
Mlle Jolie:	Oh, la Tour Eiffel est très grande. Elle est belle.
M. Grand:	Puis voilà Le Pont de l'Alma. À Paris il y a beaucoup de ponts parce qu'il y a le long fleuve, La Seine. Il y a beaucoup de bateaux pour les touristes sur La Seine.
M. Grand:	Maintenant, c'est La Place Charles de Gaulle avec L'Arc de Triomphe. C'est un quartier très élégant avec des boutiques luxueuses, des banques internationales, des restaurants et des cafés élégants.
Mlle Jolie:	Et là ? Qu'est-ce que c'est?
M. Grand:	C'est l'immense Place de la Concorde avec L'Obélisque Égyptien qui est vraiment magnifique.
Mme Petite:	À Paris, est qu'il y a un très grand musée?
M. Grand:	Oui, il y a Le Louvre. Le Louvre est un très vaste musée d'objets d'art et de tableaux. La Joconde (Mona Lisa) de l'artiste italien Léonard de Vinci est dans le Louvre.
Mme Petite:	La Joconde est vraiment très célèbre.
M. Grand:	Maintenant, c'est L'Opéra Garnier qui est un splendide palais pour la musique classique et la danse.
M. Grand:	Puis le quartier populaire de Montmartre avec la grande église Le Sacré Coeur. Derrière, c'est La Place du Tertre où il y a toujours des peintres et des artistes.
Mlle Jolie:	Est-ce que c'est un quartier très touristique?
M. Grand:	Oui, c'est un quartier extrêmement touristique.
M. Grand:	Maintenant, L'Île de la Cité dans le centre de Paris. C'est une petite île sur la Seine où il y a la merveilleuse Cathédrale Notre Dame. C'est un quartier avec des immeubles très anciens et très élégants.
Mme Petite:	Qu'est ce que c'est là?
M. Grand:	Là, c'est le Centre Pompidou qui est un musée extrêmement important pour l'art moderne. Voilà. Le tour est fini.
Mlle Jolie:	Maintenant, je sais que Paris est une ville très jolie.
Mme Petite:	Et Paris est vraiment une ville très intéressante.
M. Grand:	Oui, Paris est une ville très jolie et intéressante. Vive Paris!

Track 34

Nar:	Listen to Mademoiselle Jolie talking about the languages she speaks:
Mlle Jolie:	Bonjour, je suis Julie. J'ai quinze ans. Mon père est anglais et ma mère est française. Alors je suis française et anglaise. Je parle deux langues. Je parle français et anglais. Je parle anglais avec ma famille et je parle français avec mes amis français. En général, je parle beaucoup avec ma mère parce qu'elle est gentille avec moi. Mais je ne parle pas beaucoup avec mon père car il est très souvent absent.

Track 35

Nar:	In this track Mademoiselle Jolie talks about where she lives:
Mlle Jolie:	J'habite en France, à Paris exactement. J'habite avec mes parents et mon jeune frère Matthieu qui a dix ans. Je n'habite pas dans une maison mais dans un grand appartement dans le centre de Paris. Ma grand-mère habite à Nice et ma tante Lucie, la soeur de ma mère, habite à Paris.

Track 36

Nar:	Listen to Mademoiselle Jolie as she talks to Madame Petite and Monsieur Grand about what she studies at school:
Mme Petite:	Qu'est-ce que tu étudies à l'école?
Mlle Jolie:	J'étudie l'anglais, les maths, les sciences, le français, l'histoire et la géographie.
M. Grand:	Est-ce que tu étudies pendant le week-end?
Mlle Jolie:	Oui, j'étudie le samedi matin, mais je n'étudie pas le dimanche.
Mme Petite:	Est-ce que tu étudies avec plaisir?
Mlle Jolie:	Oui, j'étudie avec plaisir.
M. Grand:	Quelle est ta matière préférée?
Mlle Jolie:	Ma matière préférée est l'anglais.

Track 37

Nar:	Listen to our friends, Madame Petite, Monsieur Grand and Mademoiselle Jolie, talking about their favourite sports:
Mme Petite:	Est-ce que tu aimes le football?
M. Grand:	Oui, j'aime le football.
Mlle Jolie:	Est-ce que tu aimes le tennis?
M Grand :	Non, je n'aime pas vraiment le tennis.
Mme Petite:	Est-ce que tu aimes le golf?
M. Grand:	Oui, j'aime le golf.
Mlle Jolie:	Est-ce que tu aimes l'équitation?
M. Grand:	Non, je n'aime pas l'équitation.

Track 38

Nar:	Listen to this letter from a young French girl:
Mme Petite:	Bonjour,
	Je suis Laura et je suis française. Et toi? J'ai huit ans. Et toi, quel âge as-tu?
	J'habite à Versailles à côté de Paris. Où est-ce que tu habites? J'habite dans une maison qui a quatre chambres: une chambre pour mes parents, une chambre pour moi, une autre pour ma soeur, Angelina, et une autre pour mon frère, Matthieu. Est-ce que tu habites dans une maison ou un appartement?
	Ma soeur a neuf ans et mon petit frère a cinq ans. Est-ce que tu as des frères ou des soeurs?
	Je parle un peu l'anglais parce que j'étudie l'anglais à l'école avec Madame Jones. En général, elle est gentille avec moi. Est-ce que tu étudies le français avec un professeur français?
	À bientôt, ta correspondante, Laura

Track 39

Instrumental version of "Un kilomètre à pied."

Track 40

Instrumental version of "La tête, les épaules, etc."

Track 41

Instrumental version of "Moi, je sais planter les choux."

List of flashcards

A set of colour flashcards linked to Hexagonie, Book 1 can be purchased separately. The flashcards included in the pack are as follows:

1	une porte	43	un coussin	81	Carlos est espagnol.
2	une fenêtre	44	un ordinateur		Dolores est espagnole.
3	une table	45	une lampe	82	un chat
4	une chaise	46	un miroir	83	un chien
5	un stylo	47	un tableau	84	une poule
6	un crayon	48	une horloge	85	un lapin
7	une gomme	49	lundi – la lune	86	une vache
8	une règle	50	mardi – Mars	87	un hamster
9	un cahier	51	mercredi – Mercure	88	un canard
10	un papier	52	jeudi – Jupiter	89	un cheval
11	une assiette	53	vendredi – Vénus	90	un cochon
12	un couteau	54	samedi	91	un cochon d'Inde
13	une fourchette	55	dimanche	92	une souris
14	une cullère	56	le week-end	93	un poisson
15	une bouteille	57	un pain	94	une voiture
16	une plante	58	un croissant	95	une bicyclette
17	un pantalon bleu	59	une baguette	96	un avion
18	une jupe bleue	60	un pain au chocolat	97	un train
19	un pull-over noir	61	un salon	98	un téléphone portable
20	une veste noire	62	une cuisine	99	des lunettes
21	un manteau orange	63	une salle à manger	100	un parapluie
22	une chemise orange	64	une entrée	101	un ami
23	un short rouge	65	une cave	102	une boulangerie
24	une ceinture rouge	66	un grenier	103	une pâtisserie
25	un chapeau jaune	67	une chambre	104	un salon
26	une cravate jaune	68	une salle de bains	105	une boucherie
27	un pyjama rose	69	un citron	106	une poissonnerie
28	une robe rose	70	une pomme	107	une librairie
29	un crayon vert	71	une poire	108	une papeterie
30	une porte verte	72	une orange	109	une pharmacie
31	un cahier brun	73	un ananas	110	un supermarché
32	une table brune	74	une banane	111	l'anglais
33	un couteau gris	75	une cerise	112	le français
34	une fourchette grise	76	un kiwi	113	l'histoire
35	un papier blanc	77	Phillip est anglais.	114	la géographie
36	une assiette blanche		Hannah est anglaise.	115	les maths
37	un lit	78	Jacques est français.	116	le dessin
38	une armoire		Céline est française.	117	les sciences
39	une commode	79	Robert est américain.	118	la musique
40	un bureau		Sarah est américaine.	119	le sport
41	un divan	80	Hirotsugu est japonais.	120	la technologie
42	un fauteuil		Kanaï est japonaise.		

Useful resources and addresses

CILT, The National Centre for Languages

CILT, the National Centre of Languages, is the Government's recognized centre of expertise on languages. The organization's mission is to promote a greater capability in languages amongst all sectors of the UK population.

CILT
20 Bedfordbury
London WC2N 4LB   www.cilt.org.uk

National Advisory Centre on Early Language Learning (NACELL)

NACELL is the national gateway to advice, information and support on early language learning.

NACELL
CILT, the National Centre for Languages
20 Bedfordbury
London WC2N 4LB   www.cilt.org.uk

Association for Language Learning (ALL)

ALL is the major subject association for those involved in teaching all foreign languages at all levels.

ALL
150 Railway Terrace,
Rugby CV21 3HN   www.all-languages.org.uk

Brilliant Publications

Brilliant Publications publishes a wide range of books for teaching French and other modern foreign languages, with new titles being added all the time. Some of our titles are listed below. For a full list, please look on our website: www.brilliantpublications.co.uk

Chantez Plus Fort   **ISBN: 978-1-903853-37-5**
20 Photocopiable Easy-to-Learn French Songs for Primary Schools
20 songs to introduce and reinforce vocabulary for topics such as 'greetings', 'numbers', 'classroom instructions', 'rhymes and sounds', and 'weather'. Teacher's notes give ideas on how to introduce, use and extend the songs.

The fully photocopiable book comes in a set with 2 CDs. CD1 contains the 20 songs (16 original, 4 traditional) sung by French children and 13 mini dialogues. CD2 contains instrumental tracks for the 16 original songs.

Jouons Tous Ensemble   **ISBN: 978-1-903853-81-8**
20 games to play with children to encourage and reinforce French language and vocabulary.

100+ Fun Ideas for Practising Modern Foreign Languages
in the Primary Classroom

ISBN 978-1-903853-98-6

137 tried and tested activities to develop oracy and literacy skills in almost any language. Sue Cave, the author, has chosen these particular ideas due to the positive impact the games and activities have had in her classroom.

Brilliant Publications
Unit 10, Sparrow Hall Farm
Edlesborough, Dunstable LU6 2ES   www.brilliantpublications.co.uk

The Language Stickers Company

Language stickers, bookmarks, posters, stampers and teaching materials to motivate young language learners.

The Language Stickers Company
Station Road, Arlesey, Beds. SG15 6BR   www.languagestickers.co.uk

Answer key for worksheets

Sheet 1c (page 18)

1. une assiette
2. une plante
3. un couteau
4. une fourchette
5. une cuillère
6. une porte
7. une fenêtre
8. un cahier
9. un crayon
10. un stylo
11. un papier
12. une gomme
13. une règle
14. une bouteille
15. une table

Sheet 2d (page 33)

1. C'est un pantalon.
2. C'est une jupe.
3. C'est un pyjama.
4. C'est une veste.
5. C'est une chemise.
6. C'est un chapeau.
7. C'est un pull-over.
8. C'est une cravate.
9. C'est une robe.
10. C'est un manteau.
11. C'est une ceinture.
12. C'est un short.

Sheet 3b (page 41)

A: noire, verte, brune, grise, jaune, rouge, rose, orange

B: jaune rouge, rose, orange

C: bleu/bleue, noir/noire, jaune, rouge, rose, orange

Sheet 3d (page 43)

1. C'est une armoire _____.
2. C'est une lampe _____.
3. C'est un fauteuil _____.
4. C'est une commode _____.
5. C'est un coussin _____.

Sheet 3e (page 44)

1. Non, ce n'est pas une plante. C'est un stylo.
2. Non, ce n'est pas une table. C'est une chaise.
3. Non, ce n'est pas un bureau. C'est une armoire.
4. Non, ce n'est pas un ordinateur. C'est un lit.
5. Non, ce n'est pas un divan. C'est une horloge.

Sheet 4c (page 53)

B: 1. mercredi
2. samedi, mardi
3. jeudi, samedi

C: 1. lundi
2. samedi
3. jeudi
4. dimanche

Sheet 4d (page 54)

1. C'est un tableau.
2. C'est une jupe.
3. C'est une fourchette.
4. C'est une chaise.
5. C'est un manteau.
6. C'est une règle.
7. C'est un miroir.
8. C'est une cravate.
9. C'est une horloge.
10. C'est une gomme.

Sheet 5a (page 62)

1. C'est un bateau.
2. C'est un oiseau.
3. C'est un gâteau.
4. C'est un chapeau.
5. C'est un cadeau.
6. C'est un château.

Sheet 5c (page 64)

un fauteuil/ un livre/ un ordinateur/ un dictionnaire/ un lit

une fenêtre/ une maison/ une armoire/ une fleur/ une télévision

Sheet 5e (page 66)

1. flower
2. pyjamas
3. plant
4. computer
5. present
6. television
7. cake
8. book

Sheet 6b(i) (page 74)

le lit

l'armoire

la lampe

le divan

le fauteuil

le miroir

le coussin

l'ordinateur

Sheet 6b(ii) (page 75)

le salon

la cuisine

la salle à manger

la salle de bains

la chambre

l'entrée

la cave

le grenier

Sheet 6c (page 76)

1. C'est l'étoile.
2. C'est la chemise.
3. C'est le château.
4. C'est le croissant.
5. C'est la chambre de Sophie.
6. C'est l'horloge.
7. C'est le pyjama.
8. C'est la maison.

220 Hexagonie, Part 1
© Maria Rice-Jones and Brilliant Publications

Sheet 7a (page 87)

1. Non, ce n'est pas une veste mais c'est un short.
2. Non, ce n'est pas un tableau mais c'est un bureau.
3. Oui, c'est un bouteille.
4. Non, ce n'est pas un pyjama mais c'est une robe.
5. Oui, c'est une fourchette.
6. Non, ce n'est pas la lune mais c'est le soleil.
7. Non, ce n'est pas un kiwi mais c'est un ananas.
8. Oui, c'est une ceinture.

Sheet 7d (page 90)

Italy
Switzerland
Germany
Belgium
Luxembourg
Spain

Sheet 7e (page 91)

1. Le citron est sur le bureau.
2. Le gâteau est sur la table.
3. Le kiwi est dans le livre.
4. La cuillère est sous l'assiette.
5. La poire est sous la chaise.
6. Le crayon est sur le dictionnaire.

Sheet 7f (page 92)

1. Papa est dans le jardin.
2. La télévision est dans le salon.
3. La lampe est dans la cave.
4. Le tableau est dans le grenier.
5. L'ordinateur est dans le bureau.
6. Marie est dans la salle de bains.
7. Matthieu est dans la chambre.
8. La table est dans la salle à manger.

Sheet 7g (page 93)

1. Je suis Hélène.
2. Je suis Henri.
3. Je suis Anne.
4. Je suis Luc.
5. Je suis Aurélie.
6. Je suis Jean-Pierre.
7. Je suis Julie.
8. Je suis Christophe.

Sheet 8a (page 99)

C'est un garçon…
allemand
américain
anglais
belge
brésilien
canadien
chinois
écossais
espagnol
français
gallois
indien
irlandais
italien
marocain
pakistanais
polonais
portugais

C'est une fille…
allemande
américaine
anglaise
belge
brésilienne
canadienne
chinoise
écossaise
espagnole
française
galloise
indienne
irlandaise
italienne
marocaine
pakistanaise
polonaise
portugaise

belge

italienne/ canadienne/ brésilienne/ indienne

Sheet 8c (page 102)

1. Le drapeau écossais est bleu et blanc.
2. Le drapeau gallois est vert, blanc et rouge.
3. Le drapeau anglais est rouge et blanc.
4. Le drapeau allemand est noir, rouge et jaune.
5. Le drapeau français est bleu, blanc et rouge.
6. Le drapeau irlandais est vert, blanc et orange.
7. Le drapeau belge est noir, jaune et rouge.
8. Le drapeau italien est vert, blanc et rouge.
9. Le drapeau suisse est rouge et blanc.
10. Le drapeau américain est bleu, blanc and rouge.

Sheet 9b (page 111)

B: 10 + 8 = dix-huit
11 − 1 = dix
2 + 10 = douze
8 + 1 = neuf
20 − 4 = seize
4 + 4 = huit
2 + 3 = cinq
7 + 7 = quatorze
19 − 6 = treize
3 + 4 = sept
5 + 15 = vingt
15 + 2 = dix-sept
20 − 1 = dix-neuf
10 + 5 = quinze
18 − 12 = six
16 − 5 = onze

Sheet 9d (page 113)

1. un chat, onze chats
2. un hamster, quinze hamsters
3. un chien, cinq chiens
4. un canard, dix canards
5. un lapin, treize lapins
6. un cochon, six cochons
7. une vache, trois vaches
8. une souris, dix-sept souris
9. une poule, neuf poules
10. un poisson, vingt poissons

Sheet 9e (page 114)

1. des chats méchants
2. des poires vertes
3. des vaches stupides
4. des professeurs espagnols
5. des divans rouges
6. des hommes riches
7. des passeports allemands
8. des chiens intelligents
9. des bananes jaunes
10. des canards bruns
11. des chemises noires
12. des filles françaises

Sheet 9i (page 119)

la tête
l'oeil, les yeux
l'oreille, les oreilles
le doigt, les doigts
le bras, les bras
la jambe, les jambes
le pied, les pieds
l'orteil, les orteils
le genou, les genoux
la main, les mains
l'épaule, les épaules
la bouche
le nez
les cheveux

Sheet 10e (page 132)

1. Elle a une sœur.
2. Il a un frère.
3. Elle a deux frères et une sœur.
4. Il a un frère et trois sœurs.
5. Il n'a pas de frère et il n'a pas de sœurs.
6. Elle a deux sœurs.
7. Il a un frère et une sœur.

Sheet 11c (page 141)

1. mon cadeau
2. ma chambre
3. mes amis
4. mes hamsters
5. ma mère
6. mon pull-over
7. mon orange
8. mes yeux
9. mon père

Sheet 11d (page 142)

ma sœur
mon frère
ma mère
mon père
ma grand-mère
mon grand-père

Sheet 12b (page 151)

1. Il y a deux coussins et des lunettes sur le lit.
2. Dans la chambre, il y a un fauteuil.
3. Sur la table de nuit, il y a une lampe.
4. Il y a deux sacs dans la chambres.
5. Non, il n'y a pas d'ordinateur dans la chambre.
6. Il y a un coussin sur le fauteuil.
7. Il y a des fleurs sur la commode.
8. Non, il n'y a pas de téléphone dans la chambre.

Sheet 12c (page 152)

Dans la salle à manger, il y a une table, des chaises et un tableau.
Dans le salon, il y a un divan, des fauteuils et une télévision.
Dans la chambre, il y a un lit, une commode et une armoire.

Sheet 13a (page 169)

1. Julie est française et anglaise.
2. Elle a (quinze) ans.
3. Julie parle deux langues.
4. Elle parle le français et l'anglais.
5. Oui, elle a des amis français.

Sheet 13b (page 170)

1. Julie habite à Paris.
2. Elle habite dans un grand appartement.
3. Oui, elle a un frère.
4. Matthieu a dix ans.
5. La grand-mère de Julie habite à Nice.

Sheet 13c (page 171)

1. Je parle français parce que j'habite en France.
2. Tu parles italien parce que tu habites en Italie.
3. Il parle espagnol parce qu'il habite en Espagne.
4. Je parle anglais parce que j'habite en Angleterre.
5. Tu parles allemand parce que tu habites en Allemagne.
6. Je parle portugais parce que j'habite au Portugal.
7. Tu parles japonais parce que tu habites au Japon.
8. Elle parle français parce qu'elle habite au Canada.
9. Tu parles chinois parce que tu habites en Chine.
10. Il parle anglais parce qu'il habite aux États-Unis.

Sheet 13f (page 174)

1. en Belgique
2. au Canada
3. en Suisse
4. au Luxembourg
5. en Guadeloupe
6. au Maroc
7. en Algérie
8. en Tunisie
9. au Rwanda
10. au Cameroun

Sheet 15a (pages 186–189)

B: une télévision/ une fleur/ une maison/ un livre

D: 1. the letter "e"

E: 1 "est-ce que"

2. the "Est-ce que" officers

G: 1. I am = Je suis
You are = Tu es
He is = Il est

2. "Le Roi, c'est moi"

H: I have = J'ai
You have = Tu as
She has = Elle a

I: 1. "Mon" is used before masculine words in the singular starting with a consonant or a vowel and before feminine words in the singular starting with a vowel.

"Ma" is used before feminine words in the singular starting with a consonant.

"Mes" is used before any word in the plural.

2. mon chien/ mon ami/ mon hamster
ma mère/ ma sœur
mes parents/ mes amis/ mes hamsters

J: 1 Je parle
Tu parles
Il parle

2. J'habite
Tu habites
Elle habite

3. J'étudie
Tu étudies
Il étudie

Sheet 15c (page 191)

1. Quel est ton nom?
2. Quel est ton prénom?
3. Quel âge as-tu?
4. De quelle nationalité es-tu?
5. Quelle est ta/ton adresse?
6. Quel est ton numéro de téléphone?
7. Est-ce que tu as les cheveux blonds, roux ou bruns?
8. Quelles langues est-ce que tu parles? (or Quelle langues parles-tu?)
9. Est-ce que tu as des frères et des sœurs?
10. Quel est ton sport préféré?

Printed in the United Kingdom by
Lightning Source UK Ltd., Milton Keynes
139999UK00001B/10/P

9 781905 780594